CRISIS SERVICES AND HOSPITAL CRISES:
MENTAL HEALTH AT A TURNING POINT

Crisis Services and Hospital Crises: Mental Health at a Turning Point

Edited by
DYLAN TOMLINSON and KEVIN ALLEN
South Bank University

Ashgate

Aldershot • Brookfield USA • Singapore • Sydney

Published by
Ashgate Publishing Limited
Gower House
Croft Road
Aldershot
Hampshire GU11 3HR
England

Ashgate Publishing Company
Old Post Road
Brookfield
Vermont 05036
USA

Ashgate website: http://www.ashgate.com

British Library Cataloguing in Publication Data
Crisis services and hospital crises : mental health at a
  turning point
  1. Crisis intervention (Psychiatry) - Great Britain 2. Mental
  health services - Great Britain 3. Mental health policy -
  Great Britain
  I. Tomlinson, Dylan Ronald, 1955- II. Allen, Kevin
  362.2'04251'0941

Library of Congress Catalog Card Number: 98-74638

ISBN 1 84014 389 4

Printed and bound by Athenaeum Press, Ltd.,
Gateshead, Tyne & Wear.

Contents

List of Figures and Tables

Contributors

Kevin Allen is Research Officer at the University of Leeds, in the School of Sociology and Social Policy. He is also a Visiting Lecturer at South Bank University and is a co-editor of the journal *Science, Discourse and Mind.*

Tom Clarke works as a liaison mental health nurse in an Accident and Emergency Department in North London. He is currently undertaking research into the efficacy of mental health liaison services.

Paul Godin teaches sociology at City University. He has a clinical background in community psychiatric nursing and is presently undertaking a PhD study of community psychiatric nursing in Britain. Paul is a co-editor of the journal *Science, Discourse and Mind.*

Kevin Hogan is Head of Psychology at the University of Wolverhampton. He has had a long standing interest in organisational psychology and the work which he and his co-author report on in this book draws on his research in that area.

Pam Jenkinson conceived the idea of the Wokingham MIND Crisis House and took the leading part in its implementation, which she discusses in this book. The house has been open since 1991 and Pam has been concerned with both its running and the dissemination of information about the project throughout its history.

Tony Leiba is Assistant Dean, School of Nursing and Midwifery, City University. He has specialised in Community Psychiatric Nursing, the Sociology of Health of Illness and Interprofessional studies, having spent many years working with people who have presented as psychiatric emergencies.

Sarah Matthews is Team Leader of the Liverpool Crisis Service. She was the first member of staff to be appointed to the project during the early stages of its evolution, and has taken the service through from the planning to the implementation stage, with the official launch in 1998.

Sarah Orme is a Research Assistant at the University of Wolverhampton. She has worked on a number of projects concerned with crisis services, in conjunction with Kevin Hogan, and is undertaking a PhD study in this area.

David Pilgrim is a Consultant Clinical Psychologist at Queens Park Hospital, Blackburn, and also teaches and carries out research into the Sociology of Health and Illness at Salford University. He is the author of *Psychotherapy and Society*, published by Sage.

Val Radway is manager of the North Birmingham Home Treatment Service, and previously played a key role in the development of the West Birmingham Home Treatment Service, which she discusses in this book.

Shulamit Ramon is Professor of Interprofessional Health and Welfare Studies at Anglia Polytechnic University. She has studied and analysed mental health services for many years, in relation to both practice and policy, and is the author of a number of books in this area, including *Mental Health in Europe: Beginnings and Rediscoveries*, published by Macmillan.

Christopher Scanlon is a lecturer practitioner. He teaches mental health nursing at City University and works in a crisis intervention service in East London. His interests include group analysis and clinical supervision.

Dylan Tomlinson is Senior Lecturer in the Sociology of Health and Illness at South Bank University. He is co-editor, with John Carrier, of *Asylum in the Community*, published by Routledge.

1 What are Crisis Services?

KEVIN ALLEN

Although mental health 'crisis services' have become established at several sites in the United Kingdom over recent years, much of the literature that is available on these services describes a widely differing range of responses to the kinds of mental health crises that people experience. This is partly due to the fact that there has been little consensus on what is actually meant by the term 'crisis' and how such crises that individuals experience might be best resolved.

At the beginning of this book it is therefore appropriate to examine something of what has been said about 'crisis' and to briefly review the various kinds of intervention services that are currently in operation. There are two reasons for doing this: firstly, to begin to draw together what scattered literature is available; secondly, to enable those who are not already directly involved in this area, but who have an interest in mental health, to begin to make distinctions between those kinds of provision that are currently provided under the umbrella of 'crisis services' and those that tend to fall within the remit of generic psychiatric services.

Although the notion of 'crisis' has been present in discourse on mental health for more than three decades it was not until recently that forms of mental health provision that were based on 'crisis theory', began to be made available on a wider scale in the UK. As Wallcraft (1997) has noted 'crisis' is not a term that is used very much in biomedical psychiatry. The very presence of the term 'crisis' therefore gives rise to several important questions that we must address before we can begin to speak about crisis service provision, for example, in terms of its value or its 'effectiveness'. We might therefore begin by reviewing what we mean by 'crisis'. Where has this notion of 'crisis', as opposed to the terms 'nervous breakdown' or 'mental illness', come from? When did it appear in discourse on mental health, and why? What has been said about it and by whom? If not from within psychiatry, then what circumstances allowed it to emerge in discourse on mental health at the particular time that it did, and at no other time before?

It is also particularly important to consider what is said by the users of the mental health services about what, in their view, constitutes a 'crisis'. It is

1

important to do so because the implication of the use of different forms of terminology within a disciplinary area suggests a divergence in meaning and interpretation. Such differences in interpretation have wider implications for discursive practices, the ways in which mental health is perceived and regarded, the ways in which it is addressed and by whom and the ways in which it is talked about, written about, and acted upon in terms of choices made in treatment. In particular, the significance of the inclusion of service users in a disciplinary area that has, for two centuries, been dominated by a medical model raises questions about the authority of the models of mental health it proposes (Wallcraft, 1996) and about the changing status of mental health in society.

What is a 'Crisis'?

The word 'crisis' has now come to be the preferred term that is chosen by present service users and by some providers, and also by those who call themselves 'survivors' of psychiatric services, to describe what was previously known as a 'breakdown' or 'mental illness'. The literal term itself is derived from the Greek   which means 'decision'. However, it also has other more symbolic meanings according to the different traditions of language and culture. While the Latin meaning of the term is *dividing-line*, in Chinese the word is represented by two symbols one of which means *danger* and the other *opportunity* (Liverpool City Council, 1995). For many service providers and users the term has also come to be used in the context of its Chinese meaning to refer to a 'turning point'. In this way, rather than viewing a 'crisis' within the negative contextual view of a disordered state with no meaning mental health service users and service providers are able to contextualise crisis experiences in what is considered to be a positive, meaningful and therefore helpful way.

Thus, while the one usage of the term in mental health would suggest a *danger* of crossing the divide to maladaptive, mentally 'sick' ways of behaving, the other usage of the term is taken to suggest that the event of a crisis presents an opportunity for personal growth (Waldron, 1989). The event of crisis may therefore represent 'a point of transition, a point at which all the previous assumptions about one's life may be open to question and radical changes, maybe for the better' (Wallcraft, 1996, p. 190).

Gerald Caplan was one of the first writers to develop a 'crisis approach' to mental health. His work provided not only a model of mental health but also a design of specific responses to 'crisis'. Caplan considered crisis to be an individual response to a set of circumstances and introduced the notion that a specific event or series of events trigger processes that can culminate in an unhealthy response. Crisis is 'an upset in the emotional steady state which occurs when a problem is encountered which is insurmountable by customary problem solving' (Caplan, 1964). Caplan divided crisis into three stages:

1. a rise in tension as the individual becomes aware of an unresolved problem;
2. the individual's resources become exhausted. The individual attempts to seek help from others such as friends, family or professionals; and
3. the crisis results in either a healthy or an unhealthy response.

He suggested that if there could be a timely intervention in stage 2 of this process the resolution of crisis would stand a greater of chance of being healthy. The key element in Caplan's notion of a crisis service then was one of the speed of response.

Baldwin (1978) provided a pyramid model based on six levels of emotional crisis each of which demanded a different kind of response. The top layer consists of those forms of response that are considered to be a psychiatric emergency. These forms of crisis are experienced by relatively few people but typically require a highly professionalised response. Life crises, such as bereavement or traumatic stress, which appear much lower down the pyramid, are experienced by a greater number of people, but demand an increasingly less professionalised form of intervention than those forms of crisis that are higher up the pyramid.

In practice however, one individual's reactions or stress responses to a given set of circumstances, say bereavement, will be different from the responses of another; no two individuals are alike in their response. This observation suggests that such a clear cut set of divisions that Baldwin attempted would serve only to provide a convenient nosology into which we might conveniently identify objective factors and particular symptoms. Crisis is more of an individual matter than can be objectified in psychiatric discourse. What is clear from these two models of crisis is that if a crisis service is to be effective it must not only be able to respond rapidly but that it must also be able to respond appropriately according to the needs of the individual.

When is a 'Crisis' an Emergency?

In order to differentiate between a 'crisis' and what constitutes a psychiatric emergency (see Liverpool City Council, 1995) several writers have attempted to provide an operational definition of both. Thus for Dixon (1982, p. 27), a crisis is:

> a time-limited break in a person's capacity to cope with stimuli that have temporarily exhausted all of a person's problem-solving strategies ...

whereas an emergency refers to:

> external situations requiring immediate action to prevent dire consequences.

Jacobs (1983, p. 172) defines a crisis as:

> a turning point that precludes the possibility of life going on as usual ...

whereas an emergency is:

> an urgent situation that can occur repeatedly, requiring immediate action without necessarily bringing about a change in the person's life.

According to Brimblecombe (1993, p. 40) a crisis may be defined as a situation in which there is:

> an internal disturbance resulting from a stressful event or a perceived threat to self, [that] arises when an individual's usual coping mechanisms are ineffective in dealing with a threat.

This definition of crisis may be usefully contrasted with St Clair's (1995, p. 3) definition of an emergency as:

> a full psychotic episode requiring hospitalisation and intense drug therapy to reduce the danger to the individual and others.

Puryear (1980) attempts to clarify the difference by providing the following illustration. An individual enters a hospital brandishing a firearm and demands to be admitted to the psychiatric ward. Since this person clearly poses 'dire consequences for the staff' the situation is recognisable as an emergency. On the other hand, since the staff may well have been unclear as to how they should respond individually to the situation they might themselves be considered to be in a state of crisis individually.

Here it can be seen that while the term 'crisis' may be used to refer to a range of problems that might be loosely referred to as a 'breakdown', in practice its meaning and usage is very much dependent on the position of speaker. The example also further illustrates the point that what is a crisis to one individual may not appear as a crisis to another individual faced with the same set of circumstances.

Crisis is therefore a highly individualised response to a given set of circumstances. Due to the very nature of its individuality crisis will manifest itself as different levels of distress for different people. Given those two factors, the way a service responds is an important consideration.

The Emergence of Crisis Services

Until comparatively recently, when psychiatrists were 'faced with a crisis, an emergency or an uncertainty, [they] simply admitted the patient' (Ratna, 1996, p. 14). However, with the growing criticisms of established psychiatric services, the cost-orientated de-institutionalisation of mental health and the subsequent mass closures, on an international scale, of psychiatric hospitals, the demand grew for alternatives to hospital for people in 'crisis'.

What prompted the emergence of crisis services was the idea that care in the community was a more desirable approach to dealing with mental health than hospitalisation. The move toward a community care approach was brought about by a wide range of factors. The theoretical basis for the emergence of crisis services was provided by the model of crisis pioneered in USA by Gerald Caplan (1964), whose work I have already mentioned above. Rather than attacking the kinds of treatment that had already been developed in mainstream psychiatry Caplan introduced an approach that complemented traditional mental health practices by emphasising the role of preventative measures. Caplan's theories were not about treatment of psychiatric illness but about how to prevent the occurrence of such illness in the first instance. Wallcraft notes that in this way he was able to gain 'a respectable niche for crisis theory within psychiatry'. The presence of such respectability subsequently allowed finance to be made available for projects that were focused on the theory of crisis intervention and some experimental residential crisis services (Wallcraft, 1996, p. 190).

The new models of mental illness provided by Gerald Caplan in the USA together with the contributions made by Baldwin and by Goffman (1961) and Laing (1967) disputed the value of asylum and challenged the authority of the medicalised model of institutional care. The wider provision of out-patient services fostered by the post-Second World War welfare state also coincided with the advent of treatment drugs that made it possible for those needing attention to be able to cope outside the institutional environment (Busfield, 1986). As the closure of psychiatric hospitals increased in pace in the UK, and psychiatrists continued to argue for medicalised provision, there were repeated calls from 'survivors' of the psychiatric services for non-medicalised forms of asylum and crisis care (Pfluger et al., 1993), and from others outside psychiatry 'GPs, patients, carers and administrators' (Ratna, 1996, p. 14).

The Form of Crisis Service Provision

What is not clear from any of the theoretical models however, are the specific details of what is needed and the form in which crisis provision should be established. The mental health charity MIND set about addressing these issues in consultation with its local associations and MINDLINK, it's user network.

Following discussion at a MIND conference it was decided that a crisis service should be flexible, do no harm and be as effective as possible. It should offer anonymity, autonomy, including choice of treatment, provide opportunities to talk through underlying causes of distress, and take a holistic approach. It should safeguard resources from psychiatric hospitals for mental health services. A crisis service should be able to help people with their problems when they arise, offer safety, including safety from abuse for women and black people, and respect the support users give each other. Provision should be established in a familiar and emotionally safe environment and should ensure that people can withdraw from the service gradually and be linked into longer term support where desired.

Cobb (1995, p. 23) noted that what users wanted was

> contact with people who would listen to them, not be judgmental, believe what they said and understand. People wanted confidentiality, support for withdrawal from medication, and choice. Twenty four hour access was important, as was support from other users – and payment for them. Lack of support with childcare, for example, can mean that parents in mental distress, especially mothers, struggle on until they cannot continue and are then separated from their children by hospital admission.

MIND's 1995 research in Bradford, conducted in consultation with users, carers and workers, indicated that the most urgent need was the provision of 24-hour phonelines, a crisis house and a befriending scheme.

Elsewhere, Lothian Health Authority was keen to develop a response that was based on the needs of users rather than fitting a new service into any one theoretical model. They wished to adopt 'a wide definition of crisis based on the experience of the individual' (St Clair, 1995, p. 15). Crisis was subsequently defined as 'a social or medical situation which may lead to a medical emergency, and the appropriate service response would involve minimising the damaging effects of the crisis... one of the key features of a crisis service will be the ability to respond to the statement "I am becoming unwell" rather than having to wait for some sort of damaging situation to arise' (ibid.).

Types of Crisis Service Provision in the UK

There are generally three distinct forms of crisis provision currently to be found in the UK. Some services incorporate elements of all three models, others only one.

Telephone Helplines

The aim of a telephone helpline is to provide information and support to callers and to act as a gatekeeper for access to other elements of the mental health services. The advantage of helpline provision is that its location is of little importance owing to the nature of the technology. The trade-off for the greater convenience and widespread access is the cost involved, particularly the cost of training the helpline operators who are required to assess the needs of each caller without seeing them face to face.

SANELINE, which was set up in 1992, is one of many helplines that have been set up to operate out of hours. What distinguishes it from other helplines however, is the fact that it is available on a nationwide basis. At present it is open 365 days a year from 2pm to midnight across the UK, and there are reportedly plans to extend the availability of the service to 24 hours. SANELINE's view of crisis is that a crisis is when you don't know what to do. This philosophy of crisis emphasises the need for greater information be to readily available. That philosophy is echoed in SANELINE's mission statement:

SANELINE provides up-to-date information to give callers options for action and encourage them to benefit from whatever network of care exists in their own area. It also offers emotional and crisis support to people suffering from mental illness, their families and friends and information to professionals and organisations working in the mental health field. (SANE, 1997, p. 3)

The helplines are staffed by fully trained volunteers who have been first put through what is described in SANELINE's literature as a 'rigorous selection process' before they undergo 40 hours of initial training. This is 'followed by an eight shift probationary period and on-going refresher courses. The volunteers are trained, monitored and supported on every shift by paid co-ordinators, who have extensive experience in mental health'. All calls to the line are charged at the local rate regardless of the location of the caller. Calls to the service are subsidised by SANELINE. Workers on the helpline use SID (Saneline Information Database), which is continually updated, to help callers to get in touch with services in their local areas. SANELINE volunteers are trained to provide callers with information to enable them to make informed decisions, to advise them on medical and psychological treatments and to advise callers on their legal rights. The helpline volunteers are supported by a legal team comprising a barrister, who is a member of the Mental Health Act Commission, and by a panel of 150 solicitors who give callers half an hour's free legal advice. There are also a number of Consultant Psychiatrists who can be called on to offer opinion. SANELINE also offer what they call 'caller care'. This is basically a call-back which is offered as a form of 'ongoing emotional support' (ibid., p. 18). There is also local outreach support which is intended to give assistance to those who need help to access a local service, for instance those who are at risk of being isolated whether due to illness, their social situation or because of complicated admission procedures. Outreach support workers are provided with named contacts in the health and social services sector, as well as voluntary organisations, with whom they can liaise on a caller's behalf.

There are some indications that helplines could relieve the pressure on other forms of service both by providing advice and support and by helping guide people to the most appropriate sources of care. SANELINE's own research, at least, certainly appears to lend credibility to such a view. In its first year it received a total of 71,000 calls. As St Clair notes (1995), around two-thirds of these callers required information rather than referral or intervention. In SANELINE's analysis of the reasons why calls were made specifically to them, they report that 52 per cent of callers thought that the existing services in their area were unhelpful, and that their GP or psychiatrist was unable to provide the emotional and listening support they wanted. Twenty-nine per cent used SANELINE because they found that services were not available out of hours, which was when they felt that they needed support. Fifteen per cent of callers reported that they had called SANELINE because they were unable to identify appropriate local services, and 3 per cent were classified as either unable to locate a service or were unable to access them due to the length of waiting lists (SANE, ibid.).

Being a nationally available service may, however, have some drawbacks. 'A number of users of psychiatric services in Lothian commented that they were aware of the existence of SANELINE, but chose not to utilise the service because they found the London accents of the people answering the phone off-putting' (St Clair, 1995, p. 12).

Outreach

Outreach offers the opportunity of a greater level of support than can be offered by the telephone helpline alone although the disadvantage of these forms of service is that they require a higher level of human resources. Some services are available 24 hours, others are available during office hours only. Staff who are involved in outreach are professionally trained mental health workers and have to conduct assessments on the spot. Since resources are typically reallocated from the NHS Mental Health Trusts who already have appropriately skilled staff these forms of crisis intervention risk being the most medicalised, and while assessment takes place in the home, treatment may well be conducted in hospital. However some services, such as the West Birmingham Home Treatment Service (see chapter 6, this volume), aim to keep patients out of hospital for treatment as well as assessment. Intervention and treatment is conducted in the home and it is available 24 hours a day.

Renshaw (1989), citing a report by Martin, describes the Tower Hamlets Crisis Intervention Service. This service was described at the time as a rapid crisis intervention service. Given the similarity of its location it is perhaps worth comparing this earlier established form of service with that offered by Liverpool which is described by Matthews in chapter 5 of this book. As described by Renshaw, the Tower Hamlets provision caters for an inner-city multi-cultural population of over 150,000, as a professionally led outreach service that provides home-based assessment and treatment of psychiatric and psycho-social crisis. Its aim is to keep the patient out of hospital for assessment, though not necessarily for treatment. Referrals mainly come from doctors, social workers, health visitors and voluntary agencies and the types of referral range from major psychiatric emergencies to family and marital discord. The outreach team responds to a referral within 24 hours to make an initial assessment and to decide on an appropriate plan of action. These home visits continue until the crisis is resolved. Referrals for appropriate support are made in those circumstances where it is decided that long term intervention is required. The crisis team is staffed by two part-time administrators, a community psychiatric nurse, a part-time social worker and a consultant psychiatrist. The service is not available out of hours and is highly medicalised.

Crisis Houses

The aim of a crisis house is to provide support to individuals away from their usual situation for a period of time. Crisis houses tend, in the UK, to be run by users, carers or voluntary workers rather than medical staff, emphasise the social aspect of mental health crises, may incorporate an element of counselling and are really more of a provision for mental distress than mental disorder. Since professional nursing and medical support are generally not available on site, in case of emergencies and for reasons of safety, individuals who need that kind of support still need to go to hospital. In view of the increased costs and complexities involved, many crisis houses do not offer long term residential support. The most renowned example of this form of provision is that offered Wokingham MIND, as described elsewhere in this book. This is a MIND administered crisis house that represents what has been described as a form of radical separatism (Jenkinson, 1994). Certainly, it provides an anti-professional and anti-institutional complementary alternative to the traditional mental health services with a the philosophy of doing the opposite to conventional mental health services (see chapter 4 of this book).

The facility is housed in an old railway station, 'operates on the principles of freedom, responsibility and self-help' and aims to provide 'asylum, time, space, facilities, comfort, support and a listening ear' (Jenkinson, 1994). Referrals come from the Samaritans, the police, social services and hospital authorities. Professionals are banned from the Executive, none of the staff are trained and the support that they give draws on their own mental health service experience as users and carers. Lengths of stay are usually restricted to a maximum of seven days at the Wokingham Crisis House, 'but stays of a month or longer may be appropriate for people who are experiencing a life crisis' (Jenkinson, 1995).

Conclusion

Mental health crisis intervention services in the UK are still undergoing a process of evolution. The various forms of provision that are already in existence all have merit, are appropriate for different levels of crisis, and are applicable to a variety of consumers' circumstances.

While a telephone helpline is able to provide initial advice to, and assessment of, a caller in need and the rapidity of the technology has the capability of minimising distress, the use of technology itself is not a panacea. The call-back, so called 'caller care', approach adopted by SANELINE therefore seems to be appropriate and is in keeping with the consumer approach to healthcare. Some callers' needs will go beyond the need for information alone and these might be best satisfied by an integrated outreach provision or referral to a crisis centre where individuals could receive support in a sympathetic environment away from their home. Where the individual's needs are beyond the remit of the crisis centre, and demand a more professionalised approach, then ideally a telephone helpline line might pass on the referral to a rapid response team who would make the assessment and act as gatekeeper to the local hospital.

In view of the fact that crises can occur at any hour of the day or night then the availability of intervention services, whatever the form of provision, should really be on a 24 hourly basis if the intervention is to be timely and effective. Thus, while telephone helplines are a most useful and convenient way of providing information and advice to the caller and establishing the caller's needs, clearly such forms of help need to be fully integrated with other forms of crisis intervention service that are available in a caller's locality.

References

Baldwin, B. (1978), 'A paradigm for the classification of emotional crises: implications for crisis intervention', *American Journal of Orthopsychiatry*, Vol. 48, pp. 438–551.

Brimblecombe, N. (1993), 'Family crisis', *Nursing Times*, Vol. 89, No. 44, pp. 40–41.

Busfield, J. (1986), *Managing Madness*, Hutchinson, London.

Caplan, G. (1964), *Principles of Preventive Psychiatry*, Tavistock, London.

Cobb, A. (1995), 'Crisis? What Crisis?', *Health Service Journal*, 12 January, 1995.

Dixon, K. (1982), 'Personal crisis and psychiatric emergency: commentary on case mismanagement in crisis clinics', *Crisis Intervention*, Vol. 12, No. 1, pp. 24–35.

Evans, B. (1993), *Mental Health Crisis Services in Lancaster District, A report on the views of service users and carers*, Lancaster Priority Services NHS Trust, Lancaster.

Goffman, E. (1961), *Asylums: Essays on the Social Situation of Mental Patients and Other Inmates*, Doubleday, New York.

Jacobs, D. (1983), 'The treatment capabilities of psychiatric emergency services', *General Open Psychiatry*, Vol. 5, No. 3, pp. 171–7.

Jenkinson, P. (1994), 'Crisis houses should not be institutions', *OpenMind*, No. 71, pp. 18–19.

Jenkinson, P. (1995), 'Setting up a sanctuary', *Changes: An International Journal of Psychology and Psychotherapy*, John Wiley, London.

Laing, R.D. (1967), *The Politics of Experience and The Bird of Paradise*, Penguin, Harmondsworth.

Liverpool City Council (1995), *The Liverpool Mental Health Crisis Service Operational Policy*, Liverpool City Social Services Directorate/Liverpool Health Authority, Liverpool.

Pfluger, A., Minto, C., Sashidharan, S.G., Jenkinson, P., Shashoua, N., Day, S. and Ward-Panter, J. (1993), 'Crisis Services: Where Are They?', *OpenMind*, No. 66, pp. 14–16.

Puryear, D. (1980), *Helping people in crisis*, Jossey-Bass, San Francisco.

Ratna, L. (1996), 'The Theoretical Basis of Crisis Therapy', in Tomlinson, D. (ed.), *Alternatives to Hospital for People in Crisis*, papers from a Conference held at Leeds University, 18 September 1996, School of Health and Social Care, South Bank University, London.

Renshaw, J. (1989), *Crisis Intervention Services Information Pack*, Good Practices in Mental Health, London.

St Clair, R. (1995), *Research into Mental Health Crisis Services for Lothian*, Consultation and Advocacy Promotion Service, Edinburgh.

SANE (1997), *A Guide to the SANELINE Local Mental Health Helpline Service*, SANE, London.

Waldron, G. (1989), 'Crisis Intervention – a persistent theme', in Renshaw, J., op. cit.

Wallcraft, J. (1996), 'Asylum and help in times of crisis', in Tomlinson, D.R. and Carrier, J.W. (eds), *Asylum in the Community*, Routledge, London.

Wallcraft, J. (1997), 'Alternatives to the biomedical model of mental health crisis', *Breakthrough*, Vol. 1, No. 3, pp. 31–49.

2 Crisis Intervention Theory and Method

TONY LEIBA

It will be readily accepted by most people that personal crises are a fact of life; each person experiences crises and in general deals with them effectively, or at least sufficiently well to carry on with their lives. There are, however, times when a crisis seems so intense and overwhelming to the individual that the usual efforts to deal with it are thwarted and the person cannot carry on. In such cases the main focus of crisis intervention work is to facilitate the recovery process and so minimize the impact of personal tragedies. It is generally regarded as consisting of short term intervention with individuals and groups experiencing personal psychological reactions either to a major personal misfortune or to a disaster affecting great numbers of people – such as a fire or a flood. Although it is time limited it is designed to assist victims and survivors in returning to their pre-crisis level of functioning.

Theoretical Influences

Early work in crisis intervention can be traced to the practice and writings of Lindemann (1944; 1956) who offered help, as a psychiatrist, to survivors of the Coconut Grove night club fire in New York. This was a major disaster in which over 300 people were killed. Lindemann was concerned with trying to develop approaches to intervention which could maintain mental health and prevent emotional disorganisation, in these very specific circumstances of severe trauma. He proposed that the person providing the intervention has the dual role of firstly reducing, whenever possible, the impact of the stressful personal circumstances or the event, and of secondly, at the same time, helping those affected to solve their present problems, so that they become strengthened to face future crises by the use of more effective adaptive and coping mechanisms. It is for this reason that a crisis is often regarded as presenting an opportunity, as well as a danger, to the person or people affected.

Applying Lindemann's ideas to the wider mental health field, Caplan (1964) argued that when psychiatric patients attempt to deal with their problems during crises or transitions, they emerge less healthy from such crises. He suggests that crises or transitions which are poorly handled by psychiatric patients lead to subsequent disorganisation and mental illness. Caplan's crisis theory draws from Erikson's (1963) developmental psychology which offers the view that human beings grow or develop through a series of transitions. Erikson's development cycle focuses on eight developmental transitional stages each presenting a new challenge or crisis which must be successfully resolved to prevent clouding and confusion later.

Theorists such as Rogers (1961) and Maslow (1954) have focused on human beings' tendency toward self-actualization and their urge to enrich experience and expand horizons. In order to achieve self-actualization, human beings solve problems by reconstructing their goals when these have become blocked or seem unreachable during periods of crisis. The Rogerian premise of such actualisation is also congruent with the argument of Buhler (1962), that human behaviour is intentional and oriented towards seeking and restructuring goals.

A further stimulus to the development of crisis theory has been the collection of empirical data on how human beings cope with extreme life stress. Studies in this area are reviewed by Aguilera (1994) and include findings on the processes of coping with trauma, with death and with major surgery.

Drawing on these behavioural and developmental influences, Bunclark (1997) proposes that the individual experiences confusion and anxiety during a crisis and goes through specific stages of response. The initial impact of the crisis is experienced as shock with increased anxiety and confusion. The individual then becomes defensive and retreats. He or she then tries previously successful ways of problem solving and adjusting, and, if the coping mechanisms are successful, this will enable the crisis to be resolved. However, if the mechanisms are unsuccessful the individual will recoil further until the anxiety levels result in a 'reaching out' for assistance. If the individual is unable to use the assistance to find new methods of coping, or to resolve the problem by adapting and changing, then the state of crisis will continue. This state of crisis is typified by exhaustion, digestive system problems, guilt, irritability, anger and a sense of unreality and distance from others.

Types of Crisis

For heuristic purposes, crises can be divided into two groups: *maturational* and *situational*. It is important to remember that more than one type of crisis can occur at the same time, for example the adolescent who is concerned about his/her body image might also be experiencing the death of a parent. *Maturational crises* occur at transition points, the periods that everyone experiences in the process of biopsychological growth and development. Erikson (1963) identified specific periods in normal development when a developmental crisis could occur, periods marked by such events as birth, starting school, puberty, leaving home, marriage and retirement. According to Erikson each developmental stage is dependent on the mastery of the previous one, and unsuccessful mastery of one stage is likely to affect subsequent ones.

Maturational crises are periods requiring role changes. For example, when the individual grows from early childhood to middle childhood he/she is expected to become socially involved with people outside the family. When the individual advances from adolescence to adulthood he/she is expected to be financially responsible. In these situations the person is subjected to both biological and social pressures which could precipitate a crisis. The nature of the crisis is further influenced by the adequacy of role models, since adequate role models provide the individual with an understanding of how to act in the new role. Also affecting the crisis are the individual's interpersonal resources which will allow the individual to be flexible in trying out many new interpersonal behaviours in his/her attempt to achieve role changes.

Situational crises are caused by external traumatic events or by extraordinary situations for the individual that are outside his or her normal pattern of living. They are often sudden, unexpected and uncomfortable. The main characteristics of crisis associated with traumatic events are that they seem to strike from nowhere all at once, with the events threatening both the individual's physical and psychological well being, often beginning as emergencies requiring immediate action, and, in some instances, affecting large numbers of people simultaneously, thus requiring intervention with large groups in a relatively short period of time. A disaster such as a fire, earthquake, war or an aeroplane crash can leave hundreds of survivors, relatives, and friends all struggling to cope with loss. Such traumatic events may leave individuals physically as well as mentally scarred. According to Staudenmeyer and Steiner (1987), the individual usually experiences the event in at least one of the following forms: recurrent and distressing recollections of the event;

recurrent distressing dreams of the event; suddenly acting or feeling as if the traumatic event were recurring, with such actions or feelings including flashbacks, illusions, hallucinations and dissociative states; intense psychological distress at exposure to events that symbolize or resemble an aspect of the traumatic event; persistent avoidance of stimuli associated with the trauma; feelings of detachment or estrangement from others; persistent symptoms of increased arousal; difficulty in falling asleep; irritability or outbursts of anger; difficulty concentrating, hypervigilance and exaggerated startled response.

Situational crises for the individual often follow from the loss of established support, and a common response is depression. These crises can develop from loss of role and consequently the alteration of the individual's perception of his or her self. Examples of such loss of role are redundancy, bereavement, and illness.

When considering the merits of the 'life cycle' concept of crisis associated with Erikson's work, it is important to bear in mind that even the critical stages of adolescence and mid-life, which have received most attention in psychological studies of the last ten to 20 years, are far from clearly established in terms of empirical evidence. The stages which men and women go through may be significantly different from each other in nature, whilst working class life cycles can be argued to be quite distinct from middle class cycles. Bee (1994) suggests that women may attain the stage of intimacy and trust in relationships before they achieve identity, whilst the reverse may be true for men. Durkin (1995) points out that women's ideals of a family role which revolves around men often leads to later disappointment rather than the fulfilment suggested by their attaining 'mastery' of the role. Neugarten (1975) identifies an earlier family formation among working class couples as having significant implications for the life cycle approach to development.

The Relationship between Mental Illness and Crisis

This relationship requires some consideration because much of crisis theory assumes that crises are episodes which are to be expected to occur during the lives of most of us, and are not, in themselves, a reflection of pathology or mental illness. While most intervention models examine the response of 'normal' individuals to major life traumas and crisis events, it is true that the experience of developing a mental illness can be a crisis in itself, as can a relapse after a period of remission in the course of a mental illness. With hospitalisation in the NHS facilities becoming shorter for the mentally ill, and supervision after discharge being often limited to a monitoring function in cases of assessed vulnerability, there are now individuals and ex-patients who are presenting as what have been termed 'chronic crisis' patients. Pepper et al. (1981) suggested that health and social care staff find these individuals frustrating because they represent treatment failure or a drain on resources. Some neither comply with treatments nor follow through referrals, whilst many abuse alcohol or drugs. These patients represent a variety of diagnostic categories and Pepper et al. observe that the common problem among all of these patients is their acute vulnerability to stress, their difficulty in making stable and supportive relationships, their inability to get and keep something good in their lives and their repeated failures of judgement. All these characteristics result in their being susceptible to crises, and having difficulty in dealing with them.

Crisis Intervention

The minimum therapeutic goal of crisis intervention is to resolve the individual's immediate crisis and to restore the level of functioning that he or she exhibited before the crisis period. In order to achieve this goal it is essential that the therapist, or whoever is supporting the individual, makes an accurate assessment of the presenting behaviours, only deals with issues which are directly related to the crisis, and is willing to take an active and sometimes directive role in the intervention (Morley, 1967).

Aguilera (1994) outlines the specific steps involved in crisis intervention and reminds us that although each step cannot be defined in such a way as to stand out from the others, the typical intervention would pass through the following stages. Assessment of the individual and his or her problem is the first step and it requires the therapist to use active focusing techniques to obtain an accurate assessment of the precipitating event and the resulting crisis that brought the individual to seek professional help. The therapist may have to judge whether the help seeking person presents a high suicidal or homicidal risk. If the individual is thought to show a high level of danger to themselves or to another then, in the British system, referral to a social worker and psychiatrist will be required so that arrangements can be made for the person to be assessed and continuously supervised in a safe setting. This initial period may be spent entirely on assessing the circumstances directly related to the immediate crisis situation.

After accurate assessment is made of the precipitating events, the crisis intervention is planned to achieve the restoration of the person to his or her pre-crisis level equilibrium. It is important to find out how much the crisis has disrupted the person's life, and about its effects on family, friends and work environment. Information is also sought to determine the individual's strengths, the coping skills he or she has used successfully in the past, and what support the other people in his/her life may be able to offer. The therapist also engages in a search for alternative methods of coping that for some reason are not being used but could prove useful.

The nature of the intervention depends on the therapists knowledge, skill, creativity, flexibility and the nature of the crisis. The therapist should seek to help the individual to gain an understanding of his/her personal crisis. Frequently the individual may have suppressed feelings such as anger, denial, grief or guilt. The therapist, by helping the individual to bring such feelings into the open, may reduce tension through emotional catharsis. The therapist then reinforces those adaptive mechanisms that the individual has used successfully to reduce tension and anxiety, and gives assistance as is needed for the making of realistic plans for the future.

Finally the therapist and the client evaluate whether the intervention resulted in the desired effect, the positive resolution of the crisis. The therapist will want to know whether the client has returned to his or her pre-crisis level of functioning and whether the client's original needs brought out by the precipitating or stressful event have been met. At this stage a judgement can be made about whether the client's symptoms, which demonstrated ineffective use of coping mechanisms, have subsided. There will also need to be an evaluation of how far the client's coping mechanisms have begun to function effectively. The therapist will want to be assured that the client has a support system to rely on. In reviewing the changes which have occurred, the therapist will be aiming to credit the changes to the client, so that he or she can see his or her own effectiveness. The therapist will also discuss with the client how the learning from the experience of crisis that has taken place may help in coping with future crises. However, if the evaluation shows that goals have not been met the client and the therapist must, of necessity, go back to the first step, that of assessment, and continue through the stages again. If at the end of the evaluation the client and the therapist believe that referral for another type of professional help would be useful, the referral will be made.

Brief Therapy

Brief therapy has as its goal the removal of specific symptoms and of aiding in the prevention of deeper neurotic or psychotic symptoms. It is argued to be useful for people suffering acute emotional pain, severely disruptive circumstances, and situations which endanger the life of the individual and others. Its focus is on the present situation and, as is the case with crisis intervention generally, the restoration of the individual to his or her pre-crisis functioning. The basic tools used are psychodynamic interventions, mainly free associations and interpretations in a modified manner. These are techniques designed to help the person in crisis describe and make sense of how they see the events happening around them, and the events in which they are participating. According to Bellak and Small (1965) positive transference should be encouraged, it being crucial that the client sees the therapist as likable, reliable and understanding. The client must believe that the therapist will be able to help. This type of relationship is necessary if helping goals are to be achieved in a short period of time. This does not mean that negative transference feelings are to be ignored, but that the therapist assumes an active role in which the positive is accentuated and productive behaviour encouraged. The process of ending the therapy is most important in brief therapy since the client must be left with a positive feeling that he or she has begun to understand and solve his/her own problems, and that he or she may return it the need arises.

Power Issues in the Professional to Client Relationship

The views about crisis intervention presented so far are derived and maintained in relationships which are often characterised by an imbalance of power between the health and or social care professional and the service user. This is inherent not only in the usually greater psychological knowledge of the therapist, but in the investment of responsibility for social control in many 'front line' professional staff. Most notably, it is they who are given the power to decide whether a person is so much a risk to themselves or to others as to require compulsory supervision. Without good advocacy, or sensitivity on the part of the therapist, the imbalance of power can reduce the service user's self-determination, inhibiting the ability to question, to reflect, to be heard, and to be able to disagree with what is being said and done. These issues are discussed by Pilgrim in the next chapter and, as he notes, informal and unwritten 'control' rules may be as important as those which are written, with the 'hidden section' being one such informal mode of control. In the relatively new field of crisis services, it is to be hoped that more democratic and transparent forms of decision making about care and control will emerge. As Hugman (1991) suggests, in challenging the professionals' ideology that their services have the sole objective of conferring health benefit on any member of society who has the need for them, there is a need for both trade unions and professional organisations to open up their decision making on standards and ethics to wider public involvement, if change in relation to power is to be achieved.

Sociocultural Factors and Crisis

This section is in no way attempting to cover the gamut of specific ethnic and cultural factors which are relevant in crisis intervention situations. What is aimed for is an outline of some of the key issues and general principles which are involved in the provision of care to a population of people from different sociocultural backgrounds. This is of importance because such factors can and do act as barriers in the psychotherapeutic process. Firstly, there are those professionals who are from a different and unfamiliar sociocultural background to that of the users; secondly, there are clients in need of help who are frustrated when they do not receive the kind of assistance they feel they need. This frustration is sometimes attributable to issues which relate to the sociocultural background of the treating professionals. Most health and social care professionals are from the dominant European white middle class culture, and they will usually have difficulties when confronted by someone from a different sociocultural background. In these situations the language and the terminology used are a mutual problem because codes of conduct and behavioural expectations are not understood. This results in mutual suspicion with the professional feeling that the individual does not really want his/her help, and the individual feeling uncomfortable and mistrustful, and not being able to communicate. Some cultures may lay stress on predetermination, divine interventions, evil possessions and resignation to fate. If communication is faulty, culture is misread and misinterpreted leading to further alienation and fear. This point can be simply illustrated by reference to an amusing but deadly serious report by Butcher (1997) in the *Daily Telegraph* newspaper regarding Gurkha soldiers coming to Britain for the first time. The Major had to have his horse put down because the animal had suffered a severe tendon injury. Subsequently he noticed a dramatic improvement amongst Gurkha recruits who had sprains and strains in their ankles and knees. In the context of English culture, the behaviour of the recruits would seem most odd, yet it is possible that they had assumed that being 'put down' in some way was a fate which could well be theirs were they to continue showing symptoms of illness whilst in service.

It may be said that therapies generally are eurocentric, meaning that they have developed through observations and practice with white Caucasians. Guthrie (1976) described this phenomenon aptly as 'even the rat was white'. These therapies emphasise independence, individuation, responsibility and insight whereas the importance of such things may or may not be so relevant in other cultures. Non-eurocentric cultures have quite different emphases. The anthropologist Geertz (1973), for example, draws our attention to the use of teknonyms for personal names in Bali. Thus a person will be known as son of Mary, or granddaughter of Mary. This practice of naming secures continuity for the culture.

Culture and language which enables one to learn about culture and to express oneself within the culture, becomes of paramount importance when a person is under stress. The task of understanding each culture is difficult and to follow the nuances of the subcultures and their intricacies is almost too formidable to contemplate under conditions of crisis. Whatever it is one cannot deny the importance of culture. But one faces other variations in life whenever there are interpersonal transactions between people, culture being one along with gender, biological difference, ethnicity, age, social background, upbringing and life experiences. How can a therapist familiarise himself or herself with all those variations so that those fundamental issues can be considered in crisis interventions?

The Western approach to personal problems, to address them with knowledge bases accredited by scientific institutions, can easily be seen to have the aspect of scientific faith healing in this context. It is thus to be expected that many people from non-Western cultures will take a great deal of convincing that any psychiatric service is to be trusted with their personal safety.

Busfield's (1986) argument that curative individualism dominates western medicine's responses to mental illness is useful to bear in mind when thinking about methods of crisis intervention. For the goal of restoring the individual's coping skills may run counter to the goal of familial interdependence which the carers of someone being offered an intervention may believe in. A strategy of teaching coping strategies could run the risk of imposing quite alien and antisocial patterns of behaviour on the person receiving 'help'.

So it is clear that questions need to be raised as to whether or not key factors about difference can be learned by those offering crisis intervention in order to facilitate adequate service provision. But how deeply can a person appreciate a culture that they do not belong to? Transcultural theory has no difficulty with these questions, but it could be argued (Polaschek, 1998) that even the transcultural approach provides culturally unsafe practices by professionals because it does not attend to the political and the power dimensions of institutionalized practices of exclusion of the culturally different person. In this respect it can readily be appreciated that there are certainly situations in which cultural difference presents great difficulties for those service providers who are serious about responding to it. There are the situations, for instance, when professionals may believe that women's coping skills are being hampered by lack of opportunity for them to be exercised in a culture within which they are severely restrained, owing to their duties of modesty and obedience, in their actions and words.

Staff must be aware of the processes whereby they collude with institutional exclusion and so endorse and perpetuate oppression. A main strategy which can often be seen to be used in western services is the talk of ignorance. Here white workers are always saying 'we don't know how to address oppressive practices, we need more education'. Surely ignorance is not a valid justification for perpetuating oppression? All workers are morally obliged to take responsibility for seeking relevant information and to raise their consciousness. Questions which could be asked here are, for example, to what extent do white staff take opportunities, whether in the 'home' context, or during holidays and other periods away from work, to get to know about people who are ethnically different from themselves? Do white staff try to think critically about published materials which are often eurocentric, sexist, inaccurate or one dimensional in their portrayal of expectations about clients? If white staff don't ever socialize with the oppressed groups who are usually over-represented among their clients, their experience of such groups will be obviously limited. In the specific situations of crisis intervention, familiarity with a critical approach to white cultural norms and values must surely be a requirement for staff if there is to be any possibility of their addressing the central communication issues of crises.

Dominelli (1989) looking at anti-racist approaches in social work argues that staff may at times use strategies which act against the establishment of anti-racist social work. These strategies are relevant to the crisis intervention interface. Staff may use denial which is based on the idea that there are no such things as cultural and institutional forms of racism.

They may use a colour blind approach which focuses on the notion that all people are the same, with similar problems, needs and objectives. They may use a dumping strategy which places the responsibility for eliminating racism on the shoulders of black people. Finally, they may use avoidance strategies in which they accept that racism exists, but deny their responsibility to do something about it.

Conclusion

In outlining the development of crisis theory and methods in this chapter I hope to have shown how important it is to consider the context of the theory when trying to assess its validity for practice. Lindemann's early work with distressed survivors and relatives of those who perished in the fire in New York was quite specific in its nature, and designed to help people adapt and cope with great personal trauma. As the ideas were subsequently developed in relation to Erikson's work, the ability of the individual to cope with life cycle changes became a focus of interest. In this respect, it should always be remembered that crisis theory and methods revolve around the belief in the individual needing to attain mastery of successive stages of personality growth. Erikson devised his ideas before the changes brought about by the Civil Rights movement had come to fruition in the USA, changes which are still unfolding in the context of a variety of forms of oppression. Social control has been inextricably linked to the process of adaptation to life cycle changes. Maturity and mastery of early adulthood might all too easily be measured by an individual's lack of vigorous protest about their situation.

Crisis theory and method offers an approach in which diagnoses of mental illness can be held in abeyance and where the individual is assumed to be innocent rather than guilty of organic disorder upon entry to the service. It has sufficient confidence in sufferers to expect them to adapt to, and devise ways of living with, the problems that have made them so distressed, rather than bringing to bear the contents of the medicine cabinet and the manuals on disease aetiology. But there are many issues of gender, class, culture and ethnicity which still require to be addressed if crisis services are to fully exploit the liberating potential of the approach.

References

Aguilera, D. (1994), *Crisis Intervention Theory and Methodology*, Mosby, London.

Bee, H. (1994), *Lifespan Development*, Harper Collins, New York.

Bellak, L. and Small, L. (1965), *Emergency Psychotherapy and Brief Therapy*, Grune and Stratton, New York.

Buhler, C. (1962), 'Genetic Aspects of Self', *Annals of New York Academy of Sciences*, Vol. 96, pp. 730–64.

Bunclark, J. (1997), 'Crisis Theory and Intervention', in Thomas, B., Hardy, S., Cutting, P. (eds), *Mental Nursing Principles and Practice*, Mosby, London.

Burgess, A.W. and Baldwin, B.A. (1982), *Crisis intervention – Theory and Practice*, Prentice Hall, New York.

Butcher, T. (1997), 'Ghurkas mind the cultural gap', *The Daily Telegraph*, 8 March.

Caplan, G. (ed.) (1964), *Principles of Preventive Psychiatry*, Basic Books, New York.

Dominelli, L. (1989), 'An uncaring profession: an examination of racism in social work', *New Community*, Vol. 15, No. 3, pp. 391–403.

Durkin, K. (1995), *Developmental Social Psychology: from infancy to old age*, Blackwell, Oxford.

Erikson, E.H. (1963), *Childhood and Society*, W.W. Norton, New York.

Geertz, C. (1973), *The Interpretation of Cultures*, Fontana, London.

Guthrie, R.V. (1976), *Even the Rat Was White: A Historical View of Psychology*, Harper and Row, New York.

Havighurst, R.J. (1953), *Human Development and Education*, Longman, New York.

Hobbs, M. (1984), 'Crisis intervention in theory and practice: a selective review', *British Journal of Medical Psychology*, Vol. 57, No. 23.

Illich, I. (1976), *Limits to Medicine*, Penguin, Harmondsworth.

Lindemann, E. (1944), 'Symptomatology and management of acute grief', *American Journal of Psychiatry*, Vol. 101, p. 101.

Lindemann, E. (1956), 'The meaning of crisis in individual and family', *Teachers College Rec*, Vol. 57, p. 310.

Maslow, A. (1954), *Motivation and Personality*, Harper and Row, New York.

Morley, W.E., Messick, J.M. and Aguilera, D.C. (1967), 'Crisis: paradigms of intervention', *Journal of Psychiatric Nursing*, Vol. 5, p. 537.

Neugarten, B.L. (1975), 'The future of the young old', *The Gerontologist*, No. 15, pp. 4–9.

Parad, J. (1978), *Crisis Intervention: Selected Readings*, Family Service Association of America, New York.

Pepper, B., Krishner, M.C. and Ryglewicz, H. (1981), 'The young adult chronic patient: overview of a population', *Hospital and Community Psychiatry*, Vol. 32, No. 7, pp. 463–9.

Polaschek, N.R. (1998), 'Cultural safety: a new concept in nursing people of different ethnicities', *Journal of Advanced Nursing*, Vol. 27, No. 3, pp. 452–7.

Rogers, C. (1961), *On becoming a person*, Houghton Mifflin, Boston.

Staudenmeyer, H. and Steiner, J. (1987), 'Post-traumatic stress syndrome (PTSS)', *Escape Environment*, Vol. 43, p. 156.

Wallcraft, J. (1996), 'Asylum and help in times of crisis', in Tomlinson, D.R. and Carrier, J.W. (eds), *Asylum in the Community*, Routledge, London.

Wilding, P. (1982), *Professional Power and Social Welfare*, Routledge and Kegan Paul, London.

3   Care, Control and Evidence in British Mental Health Policy: The Context for Crisis Services

DAVID PILGRIM

Introduction

In the domain of mental health work, more than elsewhere, it is important to take nothing for granted. Unfortunately, far too much of the central and local planning of mental health services has contained unchecked assumptions. In this short chapter I will unpack some of these and offer some clarifications. The success of this analysis entails the reader (as well as the writer) assuming two points. The first is that conceptual analysis is as important as empirical evidence. The second is that mental health work is constituted by forms of action which require moral and political evaluation, as well as empirical verification. I approach this task assuming that facts are important but that these must be critically evaluated – their source and their utility (i.e. for whom and for what purpose?) need to be analysed. Despite the cliché, facts do not speak for themselves but are generated and legitimised by social forces. I hope to demonstrate these general abstract points by looking at practical details under the headings below.

Mental Health Care

This term has a self evident meaning to most people in most localities. It tends to mean psychiatric services backed up by social service facilities dedicated to people with mental health problems. Recently its meaning in primary care settings is being addressed. However, the three words in the phrase are all in their own way problematic. The word 'mental' for example strictly refers to internal events or phenomena associated with the mind. The latter is an abstraction disavowed by behaviourists and contested by philosophers. In the vernacular the word 'mental' is increasingly conflated with madness or stupidity (to be 'mental'). So we are not off to a good start – the first word is highly problematic, as it holds no obvious cultural consensus. The second word, 'health', when used in relation to the first, introduces further conceptual contradictions. Psychiatric textbooks contain little or nothing about healthy functioning. Whatever else psychiatrists know, they are not experts on ordinary thoughts and feelings. Mental health services are dominated by practitioners and a paradigm which are about illness not health (Pilgrim, 1997).

My own profession of psychology does not come to the rescue here either. Psychology textbooks tend to discuss abnormal psychology and normal thinking and feeling in separate chapters. Moreover, abnormal psychology is discussed in a way which is parasitical upon *psychiatric* knowledge such as versions of the DSM produced by the American Psychiatric Association (Davison and Neale, 1990).

Thus 'mental health' has become a euphemism for 'mental illness'. It does not help then to discuss an area of applied social policy with a contrary Alice in Wonderland notion. Put plainly, mental health services are not about promoting or maintaining mental health but are in practice about responding to deviant or problematic conduct. The only preventative role specialist services play could be described as 'tertiary', that is, when effective interventions prevent relapse. At this point treatment and prevention become synonymous.

This treatment-of-deviance-service focus is important to recognise when we move on to consider the third word, 'care'. This has obvious social value. Whether it refers to the State, a relative, or a shampoo, the word 'care' is alluring and positively valued – who in their right mind would want to be uncaring? We have a problem here though if we scrape the surface rhetoric of the word and the web it readily weaves for interest groups. If mental health services respond to deviant or problematic conduct, in what sense are they about care? Moreover, are the significant intimates affected by this conduct 'carers'? One dominant strand of literature refers to 'carer burden'. This conflates the concept of near relative with carer. It also assumes that carers are victims of their role and their mentally sick relatives. This dominant discourse is one dimensional and simplistic. Sometimes relatives are carers. They can also be victims of both burden and even patient violence, leading to mental health problems of their own (Rogers and Pilgrim, 1996). However, the picture is more complex than this for a number of reasons:

- some carers of people of mental health problems are not their relatives;
- some people with mental health problems are themselves carers of others (including children and elderly relatives);
- some relatives of people with mental health problems are, or have been abusive, not caring – witness the high rate of childhood sexual abuse survivors in psychiatric populations;
- some relatives who care about an identified patient may exacerbate the latter's problems during their contact; and
- relatives may be party, at times, to the coercive removal of people with mental health problems from their homes.

Thus, even outside formal mental health services, the concept of embodied care is complex – certainly more complex than the burden literature, the NSF (National Schizophrenia Fellowship) and SANE would have us believe.

Mental Health Crises

To plough on with my conceptual task, if 'mental health care' can mystify what is essentially a social control process, what are 'mental health crises'? Bean (1980) in his analysis of psychiatric hospital admissions points out that every psychiatric crisis is a social crisis. This is at the heart of the major split between the value-free discourse claimed by orthodox psychiatrists on one side and on the other their internal opposition (the anti-psychiatrists of the 1960s in Britain, France, Italy and the USA) and the later patient opposition movement which highlighted the surveillance and policing role of psychiatry. Bean's claim is incontestable, as anybody knows who works in psychiatric services. However, the protagonists within and about the social function of psychiatry would explain his claim in two opposing ways. An orthodox psychiatrist (and interest groups dominated by relatives of designated patients like the NSF and SANE) would simply argue that the 'sufferer's' illness creates crises. By contrast, the opposing view would be that all parties (the patient, their significant others and professional practitioners) play a part in creating, defining, maintaining and resolving crises. There is a third position, somewhere between, inhabited by social psychiatrists (Leff et al., 1985) and clinical psychologists uncritical of a diagnostic approach to mental health work (Fadden, 1997). This essentially argues that people suffer from mental illness and the probability of illness episodes (relapse rate) is affected by the emotional climate of the patient's family (the tertiary prevention position I noted above).

Which of the above three ways of conceptualising 'mental health crises' is applied in mental health policy does matter for service delivery style, planning and investment. This has been evident in the political ideologies associated with each and the type of empirical investigation of mental health work they have engendered. For example, a standard biomedical approach to diagnosis and treatment will want to plan services according to *professionally* defined needs – that is to say that there should be a particular number of beds, day centres and associated facilities for a particular number of patients diagnosed to be suffering from schizophrenia in any one area. By contrast, a social model of mental ill health would look to the expressed needs of *service users* in determining the type and range of facilities or support services that might be provided. The middle group would argue for greater investment in, or commitment to, community based family work (Fadden, ibid.).

The Question of Control in Mental Health Services

We do not hear much of 'mental health control' services. The term 'care' instead covers various activities, including removing liberty without trial and imposing interventions on resistant bodies. This evasion of reality by politicians and professionals about the latent control function of psychiatry is hardly surprising. If people break rules but do not break the law (the great bulk of psychiatric patients) they pose a difficult problem for all of those around them. Such conduct is a threat to the social and moral order of the day. Psychiatric patients in their depressive withdrawal, parasuicidal acting-out, or psychotic chaos, subvert an implicit social contract. This contract requires that we should all stay alive, maintain role-rule consistency, and that we should make our behaviour intelligible, when and if required, to other social actors. If all this rule violating conduct can be singularly framed as illness-behaviour requiring care, then those acting to control the deviant conduct will feel better about themselves. Those people (like the anti-psychiatrists) who dared to expose this mystification were accused of being anti-professional, anti-rational and anti-scientific (Roth, 1973).

At this point, it becomes clear that some types of reality-denying conduct lead to psychiatric patienthood, whereas other types of reality-denying conduct lead to people being psychiatric professionals. Contradictory norms also apply to dangerousness. For example, why is it that although suicide is not illegal in Britain, some self-harming people are detained without trial and given constant surveillance in psychiatric wards, whereas others are left free to kill themselves? Similarly why is that a man who is HIV positive can boast about having unprotected sex with several women, but is not constrained by the law, whereas another person who does no harm to others is detained under the Mental Health Act? This describes an actual event a few years ago in the Midlands when public health officials could find no legal means to restrain the dangerous conduct of the man. Every day, in every locality, people who are judged by professionals to be a problem to themselves or others, but are much less of an objective threat than this man was, are lawfully detained in psychiatric wards.

The judgement by psychiatrists that a person's health may deteriorate unless they are detained and treated is not then applied to a plethora of blatant health damaging behaviour. To make the point even more clear, we can highlight types of dangerous behaviour which are not legally restrained and which produce income for the government (alcohol and tobacco consumption), and other dangerous conduct which is acclaimed as being exciting and brave (taking part in car racing, rock climbing and being an astronaut). As Szasz (1963) has noted, it is not dangerousness *per se* which is the issue, it is *the way* in which one is dangerous which determines whether one is ignored, considered brave or locked up with or without trial.

A final conceptual clarification relates to the term service. This notion was constructed during the first quarter of the twentieth century. In the nineteenth century, mental health services did not exist only public and private asylums. The 1890 Lunacy Act was concerned only with defining detention criteria and clarifying circumstances of wrongful detention (all lunatics at that time were certified). The in-patient and out-patient treatment of shell-shocked soldier patients during, and in the wake of the First World War, the 1926 MacMillan Committee, and the 1930 Mental Treatment Act were important in shifting this discourse. The voluntary status of boarders in hospital was introduced as was the term 'community care' by the 1930 Act.

By the middle of the century the notion of 'service' was formally enshrined in the National Health Service Act of 1948 (although the old asylum system was nearly hived off from this reform). The subsequent mental health legislation in 1959 and 1983 continued to emphasise voluntary ('informal') status and the notion of community care was formally enshrined in a piece of legislation which applied to the whole of Great Britain and to several client groups – the 1990 NHS and Community Care Act. These legislative shifts reflected a move towards service and away from detention. However, this shift was partial not total. Much of the 1959 and 1983 Acts was about defining conditions of lawful detention and the 1983 Act actually *increased* these (the nurse's holding power).

The question is begged then, mental health services *for whom?* The parties served by civil sections of the 1983 Act other than patients are relatives, GPs, social workers and the police. The party served by the sections applying to mentally disordered offenders is the criminal justice system. 'Mental health services' explicitly and lawfully serve all of these social groups. Thus, like the term 'care', the term 'service' masks complex multifactorial processes which go beyond benign voluntary relationships responding to the expressed needs of designated patients.

By the mid-1980s, the official records of the Department of Health suggested that only 8 per cent of psychiatric patients in Britain were formally detained. However, anyone working in services knows that some informal patients are asked to go into hospital under the threat of coercion (the 'hidden section'). Also informal patients in hospital are given subtle cues that to leave might lead to immediate readmission under formal status, or to the invocation of nurse's holding powers for the same purpose. This picture is described by Bean (1986) as 'coactus voluit' ('at his will although coerced'). Moreover, with the run down of large hospitals and a shift to small acute unit arrangements within general hospitals, psychiatric wards have increasingly contained a greater proportion of formally detained patients, with locked wards having been reintroduced in most localities (the latter are euphemistically called 'special care').

The Care-Control Confusion

The habitual professional and administrative silence about the control function of psychiatry and the linguistic mystification of calling *all* of the activities of mental health workers 'care' is unhelpful in a number of ways. First, it is muddled thinking. Muddled thinking is not a good starting point to construct good public policy. Second, it is hypocritical. If mental health 'services' work some of the time in the interest of third parties (relatives, the general public, the police, the criminal justice system), then in what sense are patients being 'cared' for? Third, it does not accurately specify what are the *purposes* of services. Seedhouse (1993) has pointed out that if we are to evaluate the success of health services, their purpose must be accurately stipulated. Thus if mental health care services are *inter alia* about controlling undesirable rule breaking in the interests of social and moral order, then we need to be explicit about this in order to evaluate those services.

When large numbers of people *think* that psychiatry and its related disciplines are singularly about benign supportive relationships, which ameliorate psychological distress, and *in fact,* some of the time for all patients, and all of the time for some patients, they are about surveillance and control, failed expectations are inevitable. It explains why, when we ask service users what they think of services, they express resentment about being in hospital and being treated coercively. It may also explain why they rate psychiatrists as the *least* helpful of all the staff they have contact with (Rogers, Pilgrim and Lacey, 1993).

At this point, it is worth pointing out that the social control function of medicine is unremarkable and not limited to psychiatry. This point was made by the sociologist Talcott Parsons in his discussion of the sick role in society. Since Parsons, medical sociologists have been alert to the fact that medicine plays a key role in legitimising the sick person's right to break their social contract. However, this Parsonian point about medicine as a form of social control entailed relationships which were *voluntary.* The sick person asked for diagnosis and help. What makes psychiatry special is that it plays out its role in an unusual way within medicine – it is delegated lawful powers of coercion to impose the sick role on those who want to be left alone. With the exception of the 1983 Mental Health Act, only the National Assistance Act of 1948 allows medicine to be used in a coercive way. The 1948 Act permits the removal of people from insanitary conditions in the interests of their health. (This is rarely used and, when it is, most of the coerced patients are elderly and dementing.)

Another consequence of not unpacking the latent control function of psychiatry is that some other unchecked assumptions begin to operate. For example, one common rationale for coercive intervention is a lack of treatment compliance. In turn, this tends to be part of an amalgam assumption that mental illness is characterised by a 'lack of insight'. The latter term tends to subsume four quite separate assumptions which are run together within professional discourse (Beck-Sander, 1998): a lack of treatment compliance; deficits in psychological adjustment; poor prognosis; and the existence of a patho-physiological basis for cognitive incompetence. Beck-Sander points out that these assumptions are problematic one by one, but it is particularly problematic to use the term 'lack of insight' as a proxy for all or any of them, or to assume that one characteristic implies or is causally connected to another.

For example, whether or not a person is ill, they may have good grounds for evading medication. Most people with any sense would refuse to take neuroleptic medication – it has a high rate of life diminishing side effects, it is neurotoxic and cardiotoxic. A refusal to take major tranquillisers is thus a sensible health precaution. The chances of severe, permanently disabling movement disorders (tardive dyskinesia) increases with duration of course and level of dose. Most patients are expected to take the drugs on a long term basis, so they are putting themselves at a high degree of health risk (or the psychiatrists treating them are). Neuroleptics can be life threatening as well as life diminishing – the 'neuroleptic malignant syndrome' (Kellam, 1987). Because of the low social status of psychiatric patients, a pandemic of tardive dyskinesia has gone largely unreported in discussions of outcomes of mental health services (Brown and Funk, 1986; Breggin, 1994). Thus a silence on the latent control function of psychiatry obscures *both* the above conceptual problems (about implied lack of insight) *and* their practical consequences (some of which have meant iatrogenic disability and death for psychiatric patients).

The conjoint incorporation of care *and* control functions is not peculiar to the 'service' response of adult mental health services. It can also be found in parental care and in formal child care services. However, whereas the surveillance and disciplinary role of child rearing during a period of primary socialisation is about *children*, this is not true of adult psychiatry. Adult psychiatry represents a secondary form of socialisation, involving people of an age at which they would normally expect to be always accorded the due rights of adult citizenship. What we have inherited from Victorian social policy is a strong strand of paternalism, in which the State has delegated powers of social discipline to the medical profession, and the latter has embraced that role by using its discretion, as if it were a parent in charge of children. Consequently, medical paternalism and the infantilisation of patients became the norm in mental health work.

The challenge facing more recent mental health policy is that, for reasons of social stability, the State wishes to continue to delegate one type of disciplinary role to psychiatry but, on the other hand, it has to face new questions of citizenship which challenge medical paternalism and do not infantalise patients. This new challenge has arisen from two principal sources: political pressure from the right to promote consumerism in public policy; and pressure from the left in the form of anti-psychiatry and the users' movement (Rogers and Pilgrim, 1996). Some academic analysts of mental health work go so far as arguing that post-Victorian psychiatry has been more about producing subjectivity than controlling deviant conduct (Miller and Rose, 1988). Whilst it is true that during the twentieth century psychiatry has become more eclectic, psychologically and community orientated and voluntary in its practices, this shift has been only partial (Pilgrim and Rogers, 1994). Much of its work is dominated by biological treatment given under conditions of coercion, whilst the financing of mental health services is still given over, in the main, to hospital based facilities. What we have witnessed in recent years is more re-institutionalisation than deinstitutionalisation.

Mental health workers and their supervisors and directors in the civil service and central government are operating in a current political context of substantial contradiction. On the one hand, a vote sensitive group of politicians err in the direction of social control (the moratorium on bed closures, expensive mandatory homicide inquiries, the return of locked wards, supervised discharge and so on) and on the other hand they generate a rhetoric about community care, citizenship, patient-centredness and user involvement in mental health services.

Local managers and psychiatric professionals are clearly in a double bind at times about this tension. Should they emphasise, and devote scarce time to, a risk assessment and management role in which all patients are held under suspicion of creating another scandal and more ruined professional careers? Alternatively, should they build true adult partnerships with service users, treat them with respect, offer them choices and advocate their enlarged citizenship? It is not easy to do both at the same time, for the very reason that the care-control confusion has not disappeared with the large asylum – it has merely taken a new form in acute inpatient and community settings. Some psychiatrists are beginning to recognise this contradiction and are making pleas to remove their coercive authority from their work (Bracken and Thomas, 1998).

The Question of Evidence

I now want to move from asking some awkward pre-empirical or non-empirical questions to one about evidence. The notion of evidence-based practice (EBP) developed strongly under the last Conservative government and it has been reinforced in the new Labour administration's White Paper on the NHS (though it should be noted that mental health was not included in this paper). The rationale for evidence-based practice is that there is only any point funding a health service if it provides effective interventions. Ineffective interventions waste money and they may even be harmful. The context for EBP internationally is that health policy has been driven by considerations of cost-containment within nationally circumscribed fiscal limits.

   Within EBP there are two notions of effectiveness. Clinical effectiveness refers to professional judgements, based on evidence, that an intervention improves the health of a patient-recipient. These judgements are made without reference to costs and without reference to the recipient's views, or experiences, of the treatment (save reporting symptoms). Thus, for example, psychiatric drugs or electroconvulsive therapy (ECT) can be studied to find out whether, in the view of clinicians they reduce psychiatric symptomatology. Cost-effectiveness refers to a broader concept, as it takes into account financial costs as well as evidence of clinical improvement. It also subsumes the utility of an intervention for recipients and health costs (iatrogenic or 'side' effects).

   In the light of the above discussion of pre-empirical and non-empirical issues, a number of points need to be made about applying the EBP approach to mental health work. A framework for thinking about this application is Figure 3.1 below.

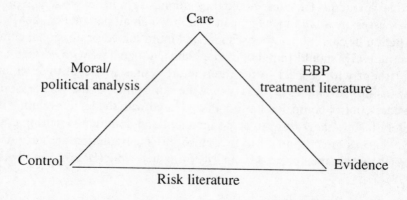

Figure 3.1   Elements of the framework for examining EBP and mental health work

   The *evidence-control relationship* can provide us with some answers about the cost-effective assessment and management of risky patient behaviour (e.g. Monahan and Steadman, 1996). The discourse about risk has tended to focus in the main on risky patient behaviour. The salience of this is amplified by the formal requirement set up by the last government, and not rescinded by this one, that an independent inquiry is required whenever a psychiatric patient commits homicide. Whilst the rate of homicide in psychiatric populations is not as high as suicide the former has warranted government prescribed independent inquiries. The professional discourse also has even less to say about a different type of risk – that of risk to patients of service contact (Pilgrim and Rogers, 1996).

The *evidence-care relationship* can provide us with some answers about the cost-effective reduction of psychological distress. The randomised control trial (RCT) approach to treatment evaluation suggests that most of the interventions currently deployed within mental health services are clinically effective. Most forms of psychiatric drug and psychological treatment seem to offer more to patients than doing nothing. (The renaissance of psychosurgery has not been based on RCTs – on logical grounds control groups are impossible to obtain.) As I have noted elsewhere (Pilgrim, 1997), we should be cautious about claiming that this endorsement about clinical effectiveness assumes cost-effectiveness. Broadly there are two problems in this regard. First, all standard mental health treatments have a demonstrable iatrogenic cost. Psychiatric drugs have undesirable effects which are life diminishing and sometimes life threatening. Psychological treatments can produce deterioration effects in patients. Second, RCTs are applied to atypical populations in atypical circumstances and they may tell us little about actual clinical services. For example, in the latter, people drop in and out of service contact, they have complex problems and they constantly interact with lay people who may ameliorate or amplify their presenting difficulties. Also, EBP based upon RCTs assumes that professionals deploy treatments competently and faithfully. In practice, therapists may not do this (they may lack 'treatment fidelity' or 'treatment integrity'). Psychologists and counsellors may abuse their patients or they may act incompetently. Psychiatrists may give drugs in overly large doses ('megadosing'), or in inappropriate combinations ('polypharmacy'). Moreover, leaving aside specific interventions, mere service contact can have health costs for patients. Becoming a psychiatric patient and entering hospital can lead to loss of tenancy, welfare rights and employment. The stigma attached to the role jeopardises future employment and personal insurance premiums.

The *care-control relationship* has to be considered in a different way to the other two sides of the triangle of Figure 3.1. Whereas the other two are essentially about *empirical* questions and answers, this side of the triangle is not. Instead, it is about moral and political values. As I noted above when discussing the care-control confusion, how mental health policy is developed in relation to the control function of psychiatry really has to be answered first by demystifying its latent character. The more care-orientated practitioners are, the more these rights of citizenship will be taken seriously. The more control-orientated they are, the more they will act defensively at the expense of patient's rights. The resolution of this tension, between care and control orientated services cannot be guided by empirical considerations alone. Service goals, specified or implicit, are value-guided not fact-guided.

Implications

Having considered some non-empirical and pre-empirical questions about the purposes and achievements of mental health services. I now want to finish with some implications.

The Care-Control Confusion is Unhelpful to Staff

It is becoming increasingly evident that a pressure to emphasise risk assessment and management is producing conservative or defensive practice. It is also creating a layer of post-traumatic phenomena in mental health professionals, who find themselves being put under the spotlight of homicide and suicide inquiries. Thus, the mental health of the mental health workforce is being jeopardised by a blame culture surrounding the actions of psychiatric patients. This is the fall-out of the irrationalities of public policy about dangerousness discussed earlier and the legacy of professional paternalism in services. For example, recently some health authorities have been sued for being responsible for the premature discharge of patients. However, breweries are not sued for being responsible for domestic violence or drunken driving, even though alcohol consumption is highly predictive of dangerousness. Service managers and practitioners operate in a policy context in which they are singled out for scrutiny about their responsibility for the dangerousness of others.

The Care-Control Confusion is Unhelpful to Patients

If patients expect benign respectful relationships and they encounter coercion, then failed expectations will lead to poor satisfaction with services and impede the development of the new 'partnership' model espoused by the Department of Health. Just as mental health professionals are unfairly being singled out for political scrutiny, so are patients. Psychiatric patients have attracted peculiar surveillance and investigatory processes. Most violence is not committed by psychiatric patients and most psychiatric patients are not violent (Monahan and Steadman, 1994) but skewed media attention (Philo et al., 1994) and biased political concern about this group unfairly raises the salience of its threat to society.

Whilst all Evidence is Legitimate Knowledge, Not all Legitimate Knowledge is Evidence

The notion of 'evidence' is narrow and scientistic. It is linked to an inadequate medical science base for health service research and the closed system of the laboratory. The organisational complexities of psychiatry, the conceptual problems inherent to psychiatric knowledge and the episodic contact many patients have with services demand a pluralistic methodology to engage with open systems. RCTs can answer some questions well but mental health service research needs also to include ethnography, organisational analysis, stakeholder interviews and deconstruction, amongst other forms of research.

Other implications could be drawn out of my earlier exploration of the relationship between care, control and evidence. However, these three highlight the connection between current policy emphases on quality assurance, evidence-based practice and risk assessment and management.

References

Bean, P. (1980), *Compulsory Admissions to Mental Hospitals*, Wiley, London.

Bean, P. (1986), *Mental Disorder and Legal Control*, Cambridge University Press, Cambridge.

Beck-Sander, A. (1998), 'Is insight into psychosis meaningful', *Journal of Mental Health*, Vol. 7, No. 1, pp. 25–34.

Bracken, P. and Thomas, P. (1998), 'Mental health legislation: time for a change', *OpenMind*, No. 90, p. 17.

Breggin, P. (1994), *Toxic Psychiatry*, Fontana, London.

Brown, P. and Funk, S.C. (1986), 'Tardive dyskinesia: barriers to the recognition of iatrogenic disease', *Journal of Health and Social Behaviour*, Vol. 27, pp. 116–32.

Davison, G.C. and Neale, J.M. (1990), *Abnormal Psychology*, Wiley, New York.

Donabedian, A. (1992), 'The role of outcomes in quality assessment and assurance', *Quality Review Bulletin*, Vol. 18, pp. 356–60.

Fadden, G. (1997), 'Implementation of family interventions in a routine clinical practice following staff training programs: a major cause for concern', *Journal of Mental Health*, Vol. 6, No. 6, pp. 599–612.

Kellam, A.M.P. (1987), 'The "neuroleptic syndrome" so called: a survey of the world literature', *British Journal Psychiatry*, Vol. 150, pp. 752–9.

Leff, J., Kuipers, L., Berkowitz, R. and Sturgeon, D. (1985), 'A controlled trial of social intervention in the families of schizophrenic patients: two year follow-up', *British Journal of Psychiatry*, Vol. 146, pp. 594–600.

Miller, P. and Rose, N. (1988), 'The Tavistock programme: the government of subjectivity and social life', *Sociology*, Vol. 22, No. 2, pp. 171–92.

Monahan, J. and Steadman, H. (eds) (1994), *Violence and Mental Disorder: Developments in Risk Assessment*, Chicago University Press, Chicago.

Philo, G., Secker, J., Platt, S., Henderson, L., McLaughlin, G. and Burnside, J. (1994), 'The impact of the mass media on public images of mental illness: media content and audience belief', *Health Education Journal*, Vol. 53, pp. 271–81.

Pilgrim, D. (1997), 'Some reflections on "quality" and "mental health"', *Journal of Mental Health*, Vol. 6, No. 6, pp. 567–76.

Pilgrim, D. and Rogers, A. (1994), 'Something old, something new – sociology and the organisation of psychiatry', *Sociology*, Vol. 28, No. 2, pp. 521–38.

Pilgrim, D. and Rogers, A. (1996), 'Two notions of risk in mental health debates', in Heller, T., Reynolds, J., Gomm, R., Muston, R. and Pattison, S. (eds), *Mental Health Matters: A Reader*, Open University Press/Macmillan, Basingstoke.

Rogers, A. and Pilgrim, D. (1996), *Mental Health Policy In Britain*, Macmillan, Basingstoke.

Rogers, A., Pilgrim, D. and Lacey, R. (1993), *Experiencing Psychiatry: Users' Views of Services*, Macmillan, Basingstoke.

Roth, M. (1973), 'Psychiatry and its critics', *British Journal of Psychiatry*, Vol. 122, p. 374.

Seedhouse, D. (1993), *Fortress NHS – A Philosophical Review of the National Health Service*, Wiley, London.

Szasz, T. (1963), *Law, Liberty and Psychiatry*, Macmillan, New York.

4   The Wokingham MIND Crisis House

PAM JENKINSON

Introduction: First Principles

The Wokingham MIND Crisis House was set up in April 1991. The philosophy behind it was to think of everything bad in conventional mental health services and then to do the opposite. Mental hospitals are remote. The Crisis House is in the heart of the community. Hospitals and clinics have bare walls. The walls of the Crisis House are covered with a thousand pictures. Mental health facilities are often cold and clinical or dirty and depressing. The Crisis House is clean, warm and cheerful and gaily furnished and decorated. Hospital wards have communal washing facilities. The Crisis House has private rooms with en suite facilities. The toilets in hospitals are not always scrupulously clean and they have cheap, white toilet rolls and unscented white soap. The Crisis House has spotless toilets, Andrex toilet rolls and Bronnley soap. Hospitals and day centres have institutional furniture – bought in bulk. The Crisis House has furniture from various periods and decades – to suit the tastes and ages of its users. Many hospitals and day centres are devoid of animal life. The Crisis House has lots of delightful pets. Conventional facilities often display out-of-date information. The Crisis House has everything up-to-date.

Hospitals and mental health facilities are dominated by authority figures – psychiatrists, social workers, psychiatric nurses, etc. The Crisis House has no authority figures. It is run entirely by users and carers and professionals are banned. Hospitals and mental health facilities are full of secrecy, locked filing cabinets, locked offices and locked rooms. The Crisis House is open, it has no secret files, offices or locked rooms. Mental hospitals and facilities are full of pressure – the pressure to take medication and to respond to it, the pressure to participate in therapies, the pressure to resolve crises quickly and thus not to take up too many resources. The Crisis House has no pressure. It is a sanctuary. People resolve crises in their own good time, heal in their own good time. There is stimulation without pressure – the opposite of what one frequently gets in hospitals – pressure without stimulation.

39

Conventional facilities are often oppressive and do not value the individual's own contribution to recovery. The Crisis House operates on the principles of freedom, responsibility and self-help. Whilst in professionally run services users are often seen as incapable of running things, in the Crisis House users and carers are totally in charge of running the service and each user's contribution is regarded as being invaluable.

Objectives and Achievements

Wokingham, which is in Berkshire, is east of Oxford and 30 miles west of London. Wokingham MIND covers the whole district stretching from Remenham in the north (covered by Oxfordshire Social Services) down to Finchampstead in the south – home of our redoubtable MP, John Redwood.

The Wokingham MIND Crisis House does actually exist! You can walk through the front door, go upstairs and get into bed. So how did it come into existence? We, a group of local users and carers, set up a branch of MIND in Wokingham in July 1988. Meetings of the Steering Committee were held in the evenings in a room at the town's Station House, which was at that time used as offices by the Wokingham Mental Health Team. One night I went around the rooms looking for extra chairs and it struck me that it was a waste of resources to have empty rooms used for nothing but storing broken chairs when people in mental health crisis were out there in desperation with nowhere to run to. We had heard on the grapevine that MIND was to be given Station House as a base when the Mental Health Team moved to new premises so I suggested to the group that when this happened we should set it up as a Crisis House. They all agreed with this proposal.

In the early days of the formation of a charity the NHS and Social Services professionals usually leave the steering group alone to see whether they can make anything happen. Then they move in as a body, in a colonising capacity, once a valuable resource is established. I explained to the steering group that the way to keep them out was to write a constitution which banned professionals from serving on the Wokingham MIND executive committee and from intervening with any guests in the Crisis House. This was agreed and the constitution duly written. Like most things with statutory authorities, their move out, and our subsequent acquisition of Station House did not happen as fast as originally scheduled. This delay worked in our favour because we set up a temporary drop-in at the British Red Cross Centre in Denmark Street in June 1989 and by the time we actually got our hands on Station House in

April 1991 we already had a keen group of befrienders and potential crisis volunteers to be one hand at the Crisis House.

Unlike professionally run services we did no research to find out how many crisis beds were needed for Wokingham District, but you have to take some account of what I believe professionals call the demographic factors. It is obvious that a couple of crisis beds are needed anywhere, whatever the area is like, but Wokingham certainly would not need the 12 beds that the women's Crisis House set up in inner city Islington has. We started with one bed and a cot and progressed to three beds and a cot by the summer of 1993, and the house has always been used as a daytime 'drop in' as well. We set up our first sanctuary the day that we walked into the House and it was occupied in our first week. We have not had the sanctuaries unoccupied for any length of time since January 1992, but neither are we having to turn local people away. This would suggest that a three bed Crisis House is the right size for Wokingham and rather than see a bigger one I would like to encourage small groups of users and carers in other areas to follow our model.

I cannot pretend that there was no struggle. I knew that there would be and there was. Nor is it a struggle that can ever be resolved because the psychiatric establishment want the power and we won't let them have it. By and large we avoided acrimonious scenes because we made no forum for debate with the statutory authorities. They are banned from our executive committee and banned from the Crisis House. They tried threatening to starve us of money but to do that they would be shooting themselves in the foot. Until April 1997 Wokingham and District MIND only received an annual grant of £4,000. This provided 30 mental health day places, round the clock crisis care for up to three people and visiting and befriending mentally ill people in the community. Even since April 1997 this grant has only risen to £6,000 per annum. At the Islington Crisis House costs are £180 per person per day because it is staffed by professionals. That is not to say that it isn't a wonderful place; it is. And the ladies using it are very happy there. At the Wokingham Crisis House costs are 180 *pence* per person per day because it is run by users and carers. Any attempt to starve us of funds would necessitate a visit on my behalf to Mr Redwood – with the relevant figures available for the scrutiny of a distinguished economist! By the stage that we have reached in the development of a voluntary organisation the statutory services have usually long since taken over – employing a lowish grade, lowish paid social worker to run the service and make use of the volunteers in a skivvying capacity. That can't happen with the Wokingham Crisis House because even if they could get rid of Pam Jenkinson they have the problem with the separatist constitution which rests safe and sound with the Charity Commission!

How the Crisis House Works

It is no good having power struggles and separatist constitutions if, battle won, what you have to offer people in crisis is no better than a mental hospital bed. The Crisis House is a 'hobbledy cobbledy' old building – *olde worlde* – with passionflowers growing around the door. It was the old station master's house and has stood there for a 150 years. This gives guests a feeling of stability and security and of going back to a time when the pace of life was slower and the pressures to succeed less overwhelming. Inside it is clean, quiet and beautiful. Guests stay any length of time from one night to several months and since we opened in April 1991 we have accommodated people in every kind of crisis. But use has changed over the years. In our early days most referrals were from the Samaritans and the Police – for people in absolute crisis who only needed to stay a night or two. Since the Community Care legislation was implemented in 1993 we have had far more referrals from Social Services and Hospital Authorities – requiring places for people who are ready to be discharged but are not ready to live unsupported or for people who need sanctuary but are not distressed enough to warrant hospitalisation. We have a crisis team composed of men and women befrienders. None of us are trained and the support that we give is based upon our own experience as users and carers.

We do guard against dangers like sexual abuse but not in the same way that statutory services provide safeguards. We do not select our volunteers, we do not train them, we do not run police checks to eliminate sexual predators. All those are professional ways of working and we do not work in professional ways! Any user or carer is welcome to join us provided that they are able and willing to keep our rules. The Crisis House is totally open. It does not have a policy of confidentiality. On the contrary, it has a policy of Glasnost! Female guests are not left alone overnight with male befrienders and female befrienders are not allowed to stay alone overnight with male guests. As many as 30 members hold keys to the house and may for whatever reason enter at any time so the cunning sex abuser who presumably works in an opportunistic way would realise that there are much more fertile fields to plunder than the Wokingham Crisis House.

In all the years since we opened in 1991, we have never had a suicide, an overdose, any self-harm, anyone sectioned from the premises, any sexual abuse

– nor any violence. That is not to say that we never could because in this life anything may happen to anyone at any time, but our record is quite immaculate and compares startlingly favourably with that of the mental hospital. The kinds of problems that we have experienced – the jealousies, the squabbles, the disappointing love affairs – are the kind of problems that you always have when you get human beings living together and I, for one, would not be without them. It is a sign of health, not ill health, when people start to take an interest in things, start wanting to make relationships, start caring about their environment and start being jealous of it. I have seen many things in the Crisis House, but I have *never* seen there a human being slumped in a chair – gazing at a bare wall having lost all interest in life. All our beautiful pictures and ornaments not only provide stimulation but also a feeling of timeless security. It would take at least a month to move Pam and her pictures out and most authorities would give up the unequal struggle.

Crisis House Features

We have an excellent mental health library of more than 200 books. This is used by the community at large as well as by our own members. Phil has been our Librarian since we opened. He suffers from agoraphobia and anxiety disorder and cannot work, which is frustrating since he is very bright. However, he enjoys his work as our Librarian and also did all the work for our successful application for a National Lottery Grant with which we bought a holiday home known as 'The Seaside Sanctuary' where our members can go for breaks and respite.

The downstairs kitchen used to be the Senior Social Worker's office when the Mental Health Team occupied Station House. We do not need an office. We have an excellent elected Secretary who also suffers from agoraphobia and anxiety disorder but is able to work and has access to modern technology. Our elected Treasurer is a carer and works as the Head of a local school. She also has access to the technology and the rest of us manage quite well on our home computers. Offices are threatening and spell 'power' to users whereas kitchens, particularly if decorated in the Dutch manner with Delft plates, spell 'mother, home and security'. Our pets are an important source of therapy for our guests. We have our own house cats, Cuddles and Shayna, but guests in crisis also bring their own pets since what will happen to them while the guest is away can be just as worrying as the thought of what will happen to the children. Our birds have their own aviary in 'The Retreat', a quiet room at the back of the house where one can just sit and have some peace and quiet and read the books of childhood.

Cuddles, the cat, who I show in photographs in my lectures, is Chief Fire Officer. Fire precautions in a Crisis House are very important and one must have the relevant number and type of fire extinguishers and check them regularly. You must also have smoke alarms and fire blankets, but, as with most things, prevention is better than cure. The Bird Art Gallery is particularly beautiful and provides a subject which is non-threatening and close to nature for Sanctuary guests. This leads to the Sanctuaries and to the Smoking Room. We restrict smoking to this one room which is upstairs so that Sanctuary guests are not tempted to smoke in bed. The ambience of the Smoking Room is masculine, horsy and doggy. It has large masculine ashtrays, bottles of whisky, packs of cards and prints of wild animals and plain leather chairs. This gives some balance to the pink frills and china ladies which are a feature of the Sanctuary bedrooms!

One of the most important features of these room is the en suite facilities. We have from time to time accommodated guests with obsessional disorder who cannot share washing facilities with others, but every guest prefers en suite and when I set up the Sanctuaries – on the principle of how I would like it if I were the guest, this feature was high priority. My colleagues say that this also accounts for the pink frills and china ladies – which just shows that no one is perfect!

Food is provided for guests who come in at a point of absolute crisis. Those staying longer buy and cook their own in this kitchen which is reserved for Sanctuary guests. 'Drop-in' members use the downstairs kitchen. We are given free supplies of non-perishable food from local schools' harvest festivals, summer and Christmas fairs, etc. We have an excellent relationship with the local community who have given us all our furniture and keep us supplied with bed linen, towels, baby clothes and equipment and with any other domestic equipment that we may need. Guests pay nothing for staying at the Crisis House. Our philosophy in this respect is the same as that of the National Health Service – that mental health care must be free at the point of delivery. Frequently guests who come in during crisis have their distress exacerbated by financial problems. By having an opportunity to come for a few months to an oasis of peace where the normal responsibilities of life are taken off them – including the financial responsibilities – guests are enabled to recover, save some money and go out on a much more secure footing – financially as well as emotionally. This is not to say that we do not believe in responsibility. On the contrary, responsibility, freedom and self-help are the philosophy on which we are founded. But crisis work involves emotional car-crash victims. We have to cut them free, let their wounds heal, and restore their driving confidence before we set them back on the road. And if in some instances we recommend the slow lane rather than the fast lane, then a change of direction is often what the opportunity enshrined in crisis theory is all about!

Since opening in April 1991, we have acted as host to well over a hundred guests, some bringing their children, relatives and pets with them. We have a very high success rate. In that time only about three guests have proved too difficult for us to accommodate and even then no violence was involved. The problem was that they needed nursing and we do not provide this. We have never had a guest who disliked staying at the Crisis House. One or two have liked it too much, but the vast majority see the great opportunity for change offered to them, make use of all our resources – both physical and human – and graduate at an appropriate time very much better off than when they came to us. Some guests do well in the sense that they jump clear of an abusive situation, but have difficulties so deep-seated that their fundamental problems are not resolved. A year later one will find them in another abusive relationship! Such guests need psychoanalytic psychotherapy and it is one of our ambitions to acquire another Crisis House for much longer stays where guests can live in a sheltered environment while undergoing analysis.

In the photographs and slides that I show of the Crisis House, I like to illustrate the way in which the House provides a good setting for guests to have friends for dinner, and to point out the efforts made to create a good atmosphere for such events, for instance by the use of embroidered table cloths and fresh flowers. If you are depressed and don't feel like eating, pleasant surroundings help. To give a graphic illustration of the importance of settings, I need only point to the experience of one of our guests who came from the Mental Hospital where she had been sectioned, having taken an overdose. I told her social worker that she could stay with us until appropriate accommodation was arranged. The social worker arranged for her to be placed in an eight foot by six foot room at the top of a doss house in Reading. The kitchen was filthy and the place frequented by criminals, drug-addicts and alcoholics. Very mentally ill men were also living in the doss house and used to wander into our guest's room in the middle of the night. She was terrified and within a day or two looked the way she had looked when she came to us from the mental hospital. Fortunately, a friend alerted me to the situation so we were able to rescue her and she stayed for some months – eventually moving to a lovely flat where she was able to resume her music teaching. You probably think that I should have made a complaint about the social worker, but I do not try to improve the mental health system and I only complain in matters of life or death. My task is to provide a better alternative so that users can vote with their feet and that is what they do!

The house rules are applied rigorously and eliminate all antisocial behaviour from the Crisis House – thus allowing guests to recover in an atmosphere of civilised peace. In seven years only one person has been banned indefinitely for being in persistent and deliberate breach of the rules. One person was banned but allowed back with a warning, and another received just a warning. The vast majority of people agree with the rules and keep them and the worst thing that we have experienced in the Crisis House is a bit of verbal aggression, and that very seldom.

So, *in conclusion*, our users and carers are happy. Criticism has almost always come from outside. I am dominating, self-opinionated, dictatorial and eccentric. None of these charges would I deny. People who defy the authorities and set up separatist Crisis Houses always are dominating and self-opinionated. Of course they are eccentric – otherwise they would be directors in mainstream services. What they would *not* be are compliant volunteers shrinking under the authority of low-grade social workers in colonised voluntary organisations! But their dominating personalities do not have an adverse effect upon the Crisis House users because they believe in their own philosophy which is one of freedom, non intervention and self-help. No guest has to have any intervention which he doesn't want. Medication may be taken or not taken as the guest chooses. Responsibility for this is only taken away from guests in absolute crisis who may otherwise commit suicide. Guests do not have to have befrienders nor overnight cover unless they want these and the use or non-use that they make of our facilities is entirely up to them. People have also queried what would happen if I dropped dead. If I did so tomorrow that might present a temporary problem, but the executive committee is very strong and would find a solution whereby the Crisis House could continue unmolested by professional infiltration.

5 The Liverpool Mental Health Crisis Service and Its Effectiveness

SARAH MATTHEWS

Introduction

The provision of emergency mental health services is currently undergoing a move away from an almost exclusively based hospital system towards one which also attempts to deal with the emergency in the community. The provision of acute services in this way can be said to have lagged behind the now well established move from hospital to community care which has happened elsewhere in mental health services, and is best symbolised by the recent and ongoing closures of the long stay mental institution or asylum. This chapter will consider one type of emergency mental health response, namely crisis intervention. It will describe the setting up and operation of a service based on this approach and will examine its effectiveness.

The Liverpool Mental Health Crisis Service is a city wide service which operates 24 hours a day every day of the year. It aims to provide high quality specialist mental health crisis intervention for people aged between 16 and 64, and seeks to support them to remain in their community, thus avoiding inappropriate institutional care.

Background

A review of general psychiatric services in Liverpool (Joyce, 1992) recommended that a working party with a suitable multi-agency and professional membership be convened to produce proposals for a crisis intervention service. The working group met during the following year and produced a specification for a crisis service. A set of first year objectives was also agreed. In April 1995 the first appointment to the Service, the team leader or co-ordinator was made. The co-ordinator's work during the first year focused upon four main target areas: research and evaluation; liaison and networking; staffing; and operation detail. Information based upon a needs assessment and the liaison and networking with all stakeholders in the city provided the basis for an operational policy and recruitment of staff. This was carried out in agreement with the working group which was now a steering group.

The Service has undergone a phased development. Phase one was completed with the appointment of the team leader. The Service became operational in May 1996 following an initial recruitment process. It was able to offer a service 12 hours a day every day of the year. Referrals were restricted to those made by mental health professionals in either NHS Trusts or the Social Services Department of the City Council, and any duty worker via the Social Services Directorate. The appointment of the remaining posts was completed in April 1997. The Service became operational 24 hours a day every day of the year. Open referrals were accepted from October. A public launch in January 1998 completed this second phase.

Defining Effectiveness

There are different ways of defining effectiveness. At its simplest there is the dictionary definition meaning to have an affect or a result. In order to examine effectiveness here the concept is defined as that of providing a service which is required by the customer. Ford and Minghella (1998) in their discussion of the evaluation of community mental health care argue that a successful evaluation, or examination of effectiveness does not simply rely on the collection of data, rather the collection exercise only becomes useful when somebody asks a question. Here there will be a definition of what is meant by a customer. This will be followed by an examination of the effectiveness of the Service in relation to this definition. In other words, this chapter will examine the question who is the customer what do they want and, if this is identified, is it being provided?

There are three main ways in which a customer can be defined. The first and most obvious refers to those who are directly affected, namely the person with mental health needs who is in crisis, their carer, relatives or significant others. The second definition refers to those who purchase and those who provide a service on their behalf. Finally, there are those who staff services. Each of these categories will be examined in turn following a brief description of the actual operation of the crisis service.

How the Liverpool Service Functions

The Liverpool Mental Health Crisis Service attempts to develop the coping mechanisms of an individual and/or family with the aim of restoring social and psychological equilibrium. The core elements of this approach include: quick assessment at the time of crisis; rapid response; direct and time-limited input (which is also subject to regular review); and the arrangement of longer term care with appropriate agencies where appropriate (Liverpool City Council, 1995a). The Service does not aim to replace those services already available but to enhance the actual response in terms of immediacy and appropriateness and then promote liaison with already established programmes of care as would benefit the service user. Intervention is offered to people whose place of residence is within the boundaries of the City of Liverpool and who are over 15 and under 65 years old. There should be evidence of a serious mental health or mental illness crisis state which could also benefit from crisis intervention.

Decisions about the acceptance of someone as a Service recipient rest with the crisis worker on duty and are based upon the information made available at referral and on the discussion between the referrer and the crisis worker. These discussions are held to establish the reason for referral and the appropriateness of intervention. Once accepted each service user will have direct access to the Service, and will be regarded as falling into one of two 'action' categories. If it is agreed that the service user requires immediate crisis intervention then they will become 'open active'. Crisis workers will aim to respond within an hour of accepting the referral. It is expected that intervention in any crisis will last no longer than a period of 14 days and will include regular review within that time. If, on the other hand, it is agreed that the service user would benefit from direct access to the Service but that they are not in need of immediate crisis intervention they will become 'open non-active'. This user 'status' will be reviewed every two months in order to ensure that information is up to date and that direct access to the Service remains appropriate.

Each service user undergoes the same intervention process. Following acceptance of the referral an assessment of the crisis is undertaken. Here the role of the crisis worker is to establish reasons for the crisis, its precipitants and to identify any risks which may be present. An action plan is then agreed which identifies areas of need and develops coping strategies using a range of approaches to enable the person to work through the crisis. Implementation of the action plan is carried out by providing support, advice, liaison and practical assistance as agreed with users and significant others. The plan can be put into action by crisis workers and/or the service user as appropriate. It is reviewed at regular intervals to determine whether continued involvement is appropriate and to agree follow up as necessary. At the closure of each intervention there is an evaluation which asks the service user, the referrer and any significant other(s) whether they have received the appropriate service and whether they have been satisfied with it.

Service Users and Carers as the Customer

Service users and their carers have long demanded a different and, in their view, more effective way of providing a response to mental health crises. Methods adopted to date are characterised by a medical approach which often results in what they describe as dehumanising, controlling and ineffectual treatment which ignores the individual and risks a detrimental 'career' in formal mental health services. The demand for a change in the way acute services are delivered gathered momentum in the late 1980s. A number of then recently formed user movements, most notably MINDLINK and Survivors Speak Out, conducted surveys among their members examining experiences of responses to mental health crisis. These surveys provided overwhelming qualitative evidence that a change in the way services are delivered at the point of crisis should be adopted. Suggestions were also made as to the core elements which should be contained within these approaches. A model for a crisis service was also included. The demand gathered momentum during the early nineties. In 1994 there was a national review by the Audit Commission of all published documents containing service users' self defined needs for mental health services. Crisis services were mentioned over 100 times. Several references about involving service users, their carers and advocates in the planning, provision and monitoring of services have also been made in the recently published Green Paper, *Developing Partnerships in Community Care* (Department of Health, 1997).

The research which has been conducted on the national level is frequently echoed by needs assessments which have been conducted to inform the setting up of local services. Recent examples include those carried out in South Tees (Kendall, 1997) and Doncaster (Merry, 1997). These assessments follow a similar pattern. Representatives of local service users and carers are asked to define what for them is a mental health crisis and in turn to put forward core suggestions for a more effective crisis service. As a result services, it is said, should allow speedy assessments, quick and effective treatments and fast action when crises arise. The needs assessment which was carried out in Liverpool was no exception (Liverpool City Council, 1995b). Here the views which were received mirrored other local, and national, findings.

A primary request is that the Service should be accessible on a 24 hour basis. The rota which dictates the working pattern for the staff in the Service is designed to enable at least two people to be on duty at any one time. In effect this means that the staff are able to visit the service user in their own environment at any time of the day or night. Telephone accessibility is available at all times. The provision of staff in this way also means that the Service is able to respond rapidly to a request for intervention. This a second, and much requested, element. The capacity to respond rapidly is also dictated by a clear criteria for referrals. This criteria is one which has been agreed by service users and carers and has a twofold function. The first is to ensure that the Service is working with those who are in mental distress and in crisis. The second is to ensure that staff are aware of the nature of the crisis, the likely response needed and the potential risks involved.

A further identified element is for a service to be offered which is staffed by those who understand the people in crisis, their mental health needs, and, in particular, the nature of a mental health crisis. For some services this has meant that they are staffed by those who have actually experienced mental health crises, the so called 'fellow travellers'. For other services this has resulted in the opportunity to employ people with either an experiential or a professional background or both. This has certainly been the approach of the Service in Liverpool. Here one of the essential criteria for recruitment is that the person has to demonstrate at least two years experience in mental health, either on a paid or an unpaid basis. The result has been that the Service is staffed by individuals who have a mix of skills and experience. This ranges from those who are qualified in mental health and general nursing, to those who are qualified in social work or have a social care background and those who have had personal experience of mental health crises. Furthermore the Service employs people whose ages range between early 20s and middle 50s. There is also a good gender balance. Finally the Service employs a staff group which reflects the cultural breakdown of the population in Liverpool. From a number of perspectives the people who staff the Service understand the person in crisis both in terms of their mental health and other needs, including cultural.

Two final observations are that service users and carers want to be involved in the decision making which informs the setting up and continuing operation of a service. They also want services to respect them and their views. There are a number of ways in which the Service in Liverpool attempts to achieve meaningful involvement. In the first instance service users have from the outset been represented on the Steering Group and have been involved in the discussions which have taken place. Some commentators would suggest that service users because they are less powerful in these settings than their professional 'peers' can only have a token involvement. In order to address this the Crisis Service has set up a service user forum. This meets on a monthly basis to receive updates on the progress of the Service, to make comments and suggestions about these and in turn feed these back to those who manage the Service and to the Steering Group. The forum is a way of trying to ensure that service users and in particular those who have actually used the Service can air their views in a setting which is less formal and more enabling. A good example of the effectiveness of this approach has been the decision to bring forward the date by which open referrals to the service were accepted. The original plan was that this should happen by January 1998. Following an analysis of the way in which the service was developing arid in consultation with service users the date was brought forward to October 1997.

Respect for the individual is a fundamental principle which underpins the operation of the crisis service and its staff. The Service has adopted a feedback mechanism which has been designed to analyse whether this fundamental principle is being met. At the closure of each intervention service users their referrers and any significant carer is asked to complete an evaluation form which asks whether the help which they have received from the service has met certain standards. One of the pertinent areas examined is whether views have been taken into account and that there has been respect given to individuals. The response is mostly a positive one. This has been analysed in more detail by an independent evaluation, the results of which are available elsewhere (EOLAS, 1997; 1998).

Purchasers and Providers as Customers

Crisis intervention and services which rely on this approach have attracted much research interest. In general this tends to indicate that these alternatives can produce outcomes at least as good and maybe better than hospitalisation. The following have been drawn from a recent survey (Ratna, 1996). Langsley in 1969 concluded that crisis admission was avoided in all emergency family therapy known to his study group and, he estimated, at a sixth of the cost of conventional care. In 1972 Decker and Stubblebine compared two groups, one receiving crisis therapy and the other ordinary services. The crisis therapy group was said to have had fewer hospital admissions, shorter hospital stays, fewer readmissions and a lower suicide rate. For Ratna, who in 1976 matched two hospital catchment area populations of 155,000, one with a crisis service and one without, the crisis population was said to experience 60 per cent fewer first admissions and 45 per cent fewer readmissions. The findings of Hoult in 1983 and Burns in 1983 also produced similar results. Ratna concludes that the unanimity of these findings is hard to ignore. The research which has been conducted on the effectiveness of crisis services indicates that the provision of acute care in forms other than hospital admission is not only effective clinically, but is less costly than an admission to hospital.

In practice the desire to look at viable alternatives to hospital admission has only become a high priority for purchasers and providers during the late 1980s and early 1990s. This has come about as a result of a number of driving forces, not all of which are associated with the clinical or cost effectiveness of the alternatives. The views expressed within the service user movement, which, as discussed above, generally come out strongly in favour of crisis intervention, are undeniably one of these driving forces. Others include the recognition of the value of crisis services by those who make government policy (they are, for example, included in the Health of the Nation's [1996] Spectrum of Care document), and the prevailing desire among NHS managers to seek cost effective alternatives to the current hospital based system.

Ratna (1997) argues that current interests in the notion of crisis have two separate orientations: firstly, to prevent mental illness as proposed in the pioneering texts; and secondly, to make up for the shortfall in acute hospital beds. It often remains the perception of both purchasers and providers that crisis services can only be effective with people who do not have a severe and enduring mental illness or where the risk of harm to others or self is low. It is argued that crisis services see a new clientele, the so called social care cases and do nothing to prevent hospitalisation for those who really need it, the so called medical cases. It would appear that the actual usage of the crisis service in Liverpool to date would indicate that this is not the case. Data on usage so far indicates that the service is used in higher numbers and for those with a severe and enduring mental illness as the result of referrals by providers in the medical and nursing field and in less numbers by those providers in the social work field.

Unlike the research which has been conducted into the cost and clinical benefits of crisis intervention, very little has been carried out in relation to its value as a social work method for those in mental health crisis. Crisis services have not been analysed in relation to their effectiveness as an alternative to hospital admission at the point of a formal assessment nor in more general terms, their effectiveness as a social work tool for use in mental health crises. The Service in Liverpool aims to maintain people in their own homes and provide a least restrictive alternative to hospital according to statutory requirements. This echoes a key objective of the National Health Service and Community Care Act (1990) which is to enable people to live in their own homes wherever this is feasible and sensible. The Mental Health Act (1983) meanwhile requires an Approved Social Worker to satisfy themselves that 'detention in hospital is in all circumstances of the case the most appropriate way of providing the care and medical treatment of which the patient stands in need' (Section 13.2 Mental Health Act 1983).

Prior to the opening of the Service, Approved Social Workers in Liverpool were sent a questionnaire to complete on all assessments for admission to hospital carried out in March 1996. This part of the crisis service needs assessment tried to establish a baseline measure for the service by identifying rates and possible types of referral. It was also a way of advertising the setting up of the Service. One of the results of this research showed that approximately 30 per cent of people being assessed would have been appropriate referrals to the crisis team (Matthews, 1995). This figure was reached by matching those assessments the Approved Social Workers said they would have referred to the team with the criteria for referral. The statistical evidence thus far seems to indicate however that there is an under use of the crisis service by Approved Social Workers.

There are a number of reasons as to why this may be so (O'Hare, 1997). Firstly, crises may be identified earlier by other mental health professionals and their intervention bypasses the need for formal assessment. It is indeed the case that a lot of referrals are received from keyworkers and care managers as a way of preventing future crises. A significant number are also received from the on call psychiatric medical staff at the Accident and Emergency Department and lately an increasing number from General Practitioners. Secondly, there may be other requirements. For example, a worker may wish to access an alternative residential facility, an option which is currently not available to the crisis service. Thirdly, the Approved Social Workers may perceive that assessments are actually taking place at a time when the crisis has gone 'too far' and that it is felt that the only alternative is an admission to hospital. Finally, the Service may not yet have overcome traditional working practice and culture. There are some 100 Approved Social Workers in Liverpool. A forum is held on a regular basis but is poorly attended. It is difficult for the Service to inform this group of what is actually on offer. Moreover until the Service is actually experienced by its referrers it is difficult to build up any confidence about the level of expertise of the team, or indeed its ability to actually offer a real alternative to a hospital bed, not least in the capacity of the team to manage risk in the community. Local research is being carried out into the role and experiences of Approved Social Workers in Liverpool. This includes an analysis of their use of the crisis service. At the time of writing data is still being collected, the results of which are not yet available. There continues to be a number of methods being adopted locally in an attempt to rectify this apparent gap in relation to the crisis service. Each Approved Social Worker has for example been asked to contact the crisis service each time they are asked to do an assessment under the Mental Health Act. This would enable a discussion to be held about the appropriateness of the referral. There is also an ongoing attempt by the managers and staff of the service to both advertise to this staff group and to build confidence. These methods will be judged as having been effective if there is in an increase in referrals at the point of assessment for admission.

The Staff as Customer

Little consideration is given in the literature to the significance of the role played by those who staff crisis services. If, as mentioned above, the advent of a crisis service can challenge the hitherto dominant medical model, it naturally follows that those who are asked to staff such services should also be prepared to work in a way which is not traditional or the norm. Crisis services which are new ventures, and set up with the specific remit of providing a crisis intervention service, therefore have a unique opportunity to not only consider the needs of their staff but to build in to its strategy such measures which allow for good staff care. In this respect, the staff group is viewed as a customer. The effectiveness of a service can therefore be judged on the way in which this is achieved.

The needs assessment which informed the setting up of the service indicated that time should be built in to any rota to allow for staff care and development. The Service must allow staff time to train together to support each other and be clear about the purpose of the work. The recruitment, training and support of staff has played a pivotal role in the development of the crisis service.

All new staff receive a period of induction. This has two main functions:

the first is to enable both new and established staff to get to know each other and to begin the process of team building; and the second is to provide an orientation to Liverpool and its mental health services. Induction remains an ongoing process for all staff. It is recognised that the crisis service is a specialist service which requires access to specialist training. To this end the managers of the Service seek to access training in particular areas such as the management of stress and dealing with risk in the community. All staff receive supervision on a monthly basis. Supervision is a two way process which aims to focus on the individual's feeling about their work, address any problems which they may be experiencing, allow time for reflection and identity ways in which the individual wishes to develop. Team meetings are held on a fortnightly basis and include a time for business, a time to look at policy and procedure, and time to look at the actual work of crisis intervention by way of a case review. Here, staff focus on a particular case from the point of view of crisis intervention models of assessment and risk management.

Staff Development

Staff development receives a high priority within the Service. Development is a concept which can be looked at from both an individual and an organisational perspective. It helps to improve the effectiveness of individuals in their jobs and, in turn, contributes to the effectiveness of the organisation. The main way which this is encouraged in Liverpool is by associating learning and development with the main work of the Service, thus promoting staff development as an integral policy objective. Development opportunities are seen as a normal part of day to day work. For example, if the team comes across a case which involves them in accessing a service hitherto unknown, encouragement is given for them to find out more about that service, and to bring their findings back to the other members of the team for their information and future reference. The same culture is adopted whenever a staff member attends any training opportunities. Here staff are encouraged to share any new knowledge, skills or values with the rest of the team. This can take place at regular weekly sessions specifically set aside for this purpose, or on an informal basis during 'handovers'.

Staff are also encouraged to make visits to other services in order to observe a different working culture and to experience an identified skill in a particular setting. Individually, each member of staff is given a development interview, which, by looking at their job description, provides an opportunity for them to focus on which parts of the job they enjoy, which parts they find difficult, and which parts they would like an opportunity to develop. These individual profiles focus on the provision of experiences for the individual to develop in their job. Regular review of these profiles enables the outcome of these experiences to be assessed in relation to the particular job and the overall context of the Service. It is not yet possible to indicate if the focus on staff development has been able to sustain the initial level of effort which has been widely documented as a feature of crisis services when they are set up. However, there has been little staff movement to date and this could indicate that staff are receiving adequate support in their role. Other measures might include an analysis of the levels and reasons for any absenteeism due to sickness. Certainly a more in depth survey of staff satisfaction would provide a clearer picture and this is an area which future analysis of the Service should consider.

In a recent publication which examined models of outreach, there is a section devoted to the Tulip Outreach Team. Tulip is a mental health care in the community organisation which operates a 'Team Case Management' approach (Gaunllett et al., 1996). The main characteristic of this team was that all team members work with all clients. Workers do not carry individual responsibility. This approach has been adopted by the crisis service in Liverpool and has come about primarily as a result of the way in which the service staffs its rota. There are at least two staff on duty at any time during the day or night to receive new referrals, undertake ongoing crisis work and ensure that the service is accessible at all times. The rota is divided into three equal shifts, all staff rotate through these. Consequently a staff member could, for example, be on a set of night shifts followed by a rest period and then a set of day or evening shifts. Given that a primary objective of the service is to offer rapid response, short term, intense and yet time limited involvement then it could follow that a referral maybe taken by someone who is able to carry out an assessment of the crisis but because of their shift pattern may not be available to carry out any of the agreed action. Similarly a referral may require a response which requires up to several visits each day. Times of visits will necessarily straddle the shift pattern. Cases are therefore not allocated. Each shift is aware of what has happened on the previous shift, is given actions to carry out as agreed by that shift and in turn provide the same guidance for the shift that follows them.

This team approach is one which, although it has come about by default, is nonetheless a major factor in the way in which staff receive support in their role. This can be explained using the same guiding principles outlined by Test

(1979). For the purpose of the analysis here I will focus on the impact which this has on staff. Test argues that a shared caseload reduces the degree of individual responsibility carried out by workers and that this, in turn, reduces the risk of stress and burnout. In a service where staff are routinely dealing with high risk cases, any method which helps staff to deal with the accompanying stress is welcome. On the whole, it is my observation as a manager of the service, that the sharing of the workload does indeed lead to a decrease in the feeling of stress. The method has however been a difficult one to recognise and learn. The path which has led the staff group to accept this has not always been a smooth one. The loss of individual responsibility for referrals can leave a worker feeling disempowered, disenabled and result in a lack of motivation. It is undoubtedly the case that a worker can feel as if they have lost control and that instead of relieving stress this sense of powerlessness adds to it.

By far the hardest thing for staff to achieve in this process of sharing workload is to relinquishing their control and to trust the colleague who follows them in the shift pattern to, in effect, take over their work. It is likely that the worker will wonder if the 'new' staff will actually do what is required. They may also wonder if the work will be carried out in as efficient and competent a way as the worker themselves believes they would do it. For the staff group in Liverpool coming to terms with having to trust and respect colleagues, most of whom they had not met let alone worked with before, has resulted in a great deal of discussion and debate in order to find a working 'level'. There are several ways in which this process has been aided. All of which need to be considered in the setting up of a similar service which adopts this approach and were clearly outlined in the analysis of the Tulip Outreach Team referred to earlier. Firstly, the Service has to have a managerial, clinical and organisational framework which can promote and maintain this culture. The Service in Liverpool has a clear management structure which is aware of the pressures such an approach can have on its staff. This is echoed by the clinical and organisational structure which encourages debate about a particular intervention and attempts to allow the staff space to disagree about an approach. Ultimately it is recognised that a decision has to be made and, where this is not possible following a team discussion then it is accepted that the managers will decide. Secondly, there has to be a method of communication which is easily adhered to and which can be relied upon. Records are made by crisis workers for each contact with or about service users. These contact sheets are the main tool for communication in written form and are the vehicle for handovers in person at the beginning and end of each shift. Work is carried out to encourage consistency in the completion of these records. Finally, an environment has to exist where the worker feels safe enough to challenge and be challenged. For staff who are used to a more traditional case management approach where work is normally carried out on an individual basis and shared only with an immediate supervisor, there needs to be a fundamental shift in working practice and culture. All work is under scrutiny and open to dissection in a very public way. Errors, as well as good working practice are all subject to the same treatment. A worker has therefore to feel very confident in their abilities and in their capacity to admit a lack of knowledge or particular skill on occasion. This is managed in Liverpool in a number of ways most notably in the promotion of such a working culture by the immediate managers of the Service and also in the acknowledgement that differences will occur and will have to be resolved and not ignored. This can prove to be quite a challenge for those managing the situation and involves a good deal of hands on work in the decision making and problem solving processes.

Another more recent study conducted into what staff want from crisis services (Hogan and Orme, 1997) suggests among the other elements discussed above that staff want a clear safety procedure. In Liverpool the Service provides this in a number of ways. It is for example the norm that all visits are carried out in twos and that staff should inform a manager where they are going and when they are due back. Should they not inform a manager of their safe return then there will be a follow up to establish a reason for a delayed return. If no contact can be made there local police will carry out further investigations. Staff carry mobile telephones with them at all times and are clearly instructed that if they find themselves in a situation which is vulnerable or presenting risk to themselves, then they should withdraw as soon as possible.

Conclusion

The concept of the effectiveness of crisis services has been examined here in relation to the customer. It is suggested that an effective crisis service can be assessed by its capacity to research what the customer wants and, if identified, to provide it This chapter has focused on one crisis service, namely, the Liverpool Mental Health Crisis Service and has examined three types of customer. In two of these, where the customer is defined as the service user or staff, the Service can be said to be effective. In the analysis given it is argued that what the customer wants is being provided. In the third definition, where the customer is the purchaser or provider, it is less easy to argue that the

Service is being effective. Where it is concluded that effectiveness is not being achieved according to the original definition then the Service has to revisit the research. It needs to he sure that what was identified originally as being required is still the case. If this is not so then it has to consider the development of a different strategy. Where it is concluded that the need is as first identified the Service has then to approach the customer and try to resolve the situation. The process of examination is therefore a continuous one but it can be argued an essential element in any effective service.

References

Audit Commission (1994), *Finding a place: A Review of Mental Health Services for Adults*, HMSO, London.

Burns, T., Beadsmoore, A., Bhat, A.V., Oliver, A. and Mathers, C. (1993), 'A Controlled Trial of Home Based Acute Psychiatric Services', *British Journal of Psychiatry*, Vol. 163, pp. 49–68.

Caplan, G. (1964), *Principles of Preventive Psychiatry*, Tavistock, London.

Cobb, A. (1995), *MIND'S Model of a 24 hour Crisis Service*, MIND, London.

Decker, J. and Stubblebine, M. (1972), 'Crisis Intervention and Prevention of Psychiatric Disability: A Follow Up Study', *American Journal of Psychiatry*, Vol. 129, No. 6, pp. 725–30.

Department of Health (1995), *Building Bridges*, HMSO, London.

Department of Health (1996), *The Spectrum of Care: Local Services for People with Mental Health Problems*, Department of Health, Leeds.

Department of Health (1997), *Developing Partnerships in Community Care*, HMSO, London.

EOLAS (1997), *Liverpool Mental Health Crisis Service: First Year Evaluation Report*, unpublished.

EOLAS (1998), *Liverpool Mental Health Crisis Service: Second Year and Final Evaluation Report*, unpublished.

Ford, R. and Minghella, E. (1998), 'Evaluating Community Mental Health Care', in Brooker, C. and Repper, J. (eds), *Serious Mental Health Problems in the Community: Practice, Policy and Research*, Bailliere Tindal, London.

Gaunllett, N., Ford, R. and Muijen, M. (1996), *Teamwork Models of Outreach in an Urban Multi Cultural Setting*, Sainsbury Centre for Mental Health, London.

Hogan, K. and Orme, S. (1997), 'The effectiveness of Crisis Services: A Review of Research', Proceedings of the 2nd Annual Conference on Crisis Services, School of Health and Social Care, South Bank University, London.

Hoult, J. (1983), *Psychiatric Hospital Versus Community Treatment: A Controlled Study*, Department of Health, New South Wales, Sydney.

Joyce, L. (1992), *Review of General Psychiatric Services*, unpublished.

Kendall, M. (1997), *Time for a Change. A Feasibility Report to Identify Appropriate Crisis Services*, unpublished.

Langsley, D.G., Flomenhaft, K. and Machotka, P. (1969), 'Follow-Up Evaluations of Family Crisis Therapy', *American Journal of Orthopsychiatry*, Vol. 39, pp. 753–9.

Liverpool City Council (1995a), *The Liverpool Mental Health Crisis Service Operational Policy*, unpublished.

Liverpool City Council (1995b), *The Liverpool Mental Health Crisis Service Needs Assessment*, unpublished.

Liverpool City Council (1996), *The Liverpool Mental Health Crisis Service and ASW Assessments*, unpublished.

Merry, M. (1997), *Mental Health Out of Hours Crisis Intervention Services in Doncaster*, Doncaster Community Health Council, Doncaster.

Mitchell, R. (1983), 'Mental Health Social Work Practice: The Barnet Model', in Cohen, J. and Ramon, S. (eds), *Social Work and the Mental Health Act*, British Association of Social Work Publications, Birmingham.

O'Hare, P. (1997), Unpublished Research Proposal.

Phelan, M., Strathdee, G. and Thornicroft, G. (eds) (1995), *Emergency Mental Health Services*, Cambridge University Press, Cambridge.

Punukollu, R. (ed.) (1994), *Recent Advances in Crisis Intervention*, International Institute of Crisis Intervention and Community Psychiatry Publications, Huddersfield.

Ratna, L. (1996), 'The Theoretical Basis of Crisis Therapy', in Tomlinson, D. (ed.), *Alternatives to Hospital for People in Crisis*, Papers from a Conference held at Leeds University, School of Health and Social Care, South Bank University, London.

Ratna, L. (1997), 'Alternatives to the Biomedical Model of Mental Health Crisis', *Breakthrough*, Vol. 1, No. 3.

Renshaw, J. (ed.) (1989), *Crisis Intervention Services Information Pack*, Good Practices in Mental Health, London.

Test, M. (1979), 'Continuity of Care in Community Treatment', in Stein, L. (ed.), *Community Support Systems for the Long Term Patient*, Jossey Bass, San Francisco.

Value for Money Unit (1997), *Mental Health Crisis Services Directory*, Welsh Health Common Services Authority, Cardiff.

6 West Birmingham Home Treatment Service: 'Right at Home'

VAL RADWAY

Introduction

Psychiatric care for people with acute mental health problems remains largely hospital based. The closure of large institutions has meant the diversion of services into small units within District General Hospitals. Treatment largely retains its medical emphasis and there is rarely an alternative to hospital admission for an acute crisis. The bulk of the mental health budget remains tied up in the provision of hospital based services: during the 1980s the resources spent on in-patient services increased in real terms and there was only a marginal reduction in the proportion of health and social services spending devoted to it (Morgan, 1993). The NHS and Community Care Act, introduced in April 1993, aimed to provide a wider choice of services for people with mental health difficulties. One of the principal ideas of the legislation was to transfer money from institutional care to community care, in order to support the development of more appropriate services. However, little significant change has taken place.

Service users continue to be dissatisfied with traditional psychiatric services. When they have been asked what they would like to see in place, some of the service options they have requested include: crisis intervention teams which are available at all times of day and night; crisis houses to have recourse to at times of distress; services that are based away from the hospital; and a range of practical (i.e. non psychiatric) supports (Rogers, Pilgrim and Lacey, 1993). These proposals indicate a desire on behalf of users for a more holistic approach to care. In respect of the desire for practical support, our experience reflects the findings of the Audit Commission (1994), that poverty and inadequate housing are common experiences of people with mental health problems.

Services for People from Black and Ethnic Minority Communities

The black community has not been well served by traditional hospital based services and there is widespread mistrust of such services. Hostility leads to rejection of what is on offer and noncompliance with treatment, usually of the physical sort, can lead mental health professionals to engage in coercive practices to ensure people they perceive as ill and potentially dangerous receive treatment that they are fundamentally opposed to. In the minds of many patients from the local black communities in West Birmingham, the psychiatric hospital that they often found themselves in was no different in nature from the local prison which shares its boundary walls. Many believe, correctly, that black people are more likely than white people to be put in a psychiatric hospital and that people who are not mentally ill can be put in hospital and told they are mentally ill. Thus mental health care has become synonymous with social control and custodial interventions. It is for this reason that even if someone has been identified to have a mental health problem by people within the black community, they may well seek help, in the first instance, from alternative sources such as a religious leader or a local healer, rather than from the psychiatric facility. The character and accessibility of the available helping agencies will also influence who/what is considered by the individual or their relative to be the solution to the disturbed person's behaviour (Francis et al., 1993).

The admission to hospital represents the start of a treatment episode to the staff but, to the individual and their relatives, it is the culmination of increasing sufferings which could have been relieved earlier if help was readily available to people, help which was acceptable and easily accessible to minority ethnic peoples. It is commonly believed that people seeking help in a psychiatric crisis will utilise the diversity of pathways within the health service and that most will begin by seeking help through their General Practitioner. However, minority ethnic groups and, in particular, African-Caribbean people, are more likely to access the psychiatric services through other agencies, for example the police or social services. A number of now well reported studies have established that black people, and in particular those who are African-Caribbean, are two to three times more likely than white people to be detained under compulsory orders (Littlewood and Lipsedge, 1981; 1982). They are more likely to be removed by the police to a place of safety under Section 136 of the Mental Health Act; be compulsorily detained under Sections 2, 3, and 4 of the Act; be diagnosed as suffering from schizophrenia, or other forms of psychotic illness; be detained in locked wards of psychiatric hospitals, and to be given higher doses of medication. Furthermore, they are less likely than white people to receive appropriate and acceptable diagnosis or treatment for possible mental illness at an early stage, or to receive treatments such as psychotherapy and counselling (Department of Health – DoH, 1992).

In some cases hospital admission may give temporary relief to both the individual and the families, but before long the person is back at home, where either apathy or unpredictability may give cause for concern and the long or short wait for a relapse commences. If the sufferer is not treated the risk increases of him or her becoming more severely ill and thus precipitating a social crisis (either within the family or in a public setting). If there is a crisis, a 'section' admission involving compulsory detention in hospital becomes more likely. Over reliance on the use of in-patient facilities to deal with acute mental illness/distress creates the problem of pathologising the many interpersonal stresses which may have precipitated the signs and symptoms that led to hospitalisation. These are often ignored or not adequately dealt with and so persist to precipitate further relapses, which continue to be dealt with only in terms of psychopathology.

The Development of the Home Treatment Service

It was against this backdrop of growing dissatisfaction with local provisions, along with the ever increasing numbers of black people on the acute admission wards, that it became necessary for the psychiatric services in Birmingham to seek alternatives to hospital admission. The social and political climate at a national level also played a major role, with new initiatives emerging around the UK which aimed to provide quite distinct alternatives to hospital admission. The West Birmingham Home Treatment Service was conceived as one such an initiative. The separation of then purchaser and provider roles within the NHS, following the reforms of 1990, made it possible for the then West Birmingham Health Authority to translate the research evidence on alternatives to hospital into practice. Most studies carried out in the last 20 years which have compared non-hospital with hospital psychiatric treatment, have found the former to be as good as or better than the latter, and usually cheaper. There is not even one instance, in any of these studies, where hospital treatment has been found to be superior to community treatment for the patient, yet centuries of culturally sanctioned expectations are a powerful force and are not easily modified. An attitude of 'out of sight out of mind' is pervasive, and therefore alternatives to psychiatric hospitalisation tend to be regarded as unacceptable only because they run contrary to conventional wisdom.

The Home Treatment Service provided the opportunity to challenge such widely held views by providing a service acceptable to the local community. This meant working closely with relatives and carers, and with local black-led organisations and religious leaders, with the aim being to give 'customer satisfaction', to capitalise on the political mood of the moment. However, this method of working did not, by itself, address inequality or discrimination in mental health services – it simply amplified it. During the early stage of the initial project a certain amount of ambivalence, even resistance from other colleagues and some clients was evident. Some professionals were reluctant to change, especially when the change meant relinquishing or sharing power.

The team was set up with the support of the health authority as purchasers of mental health care for the local area. Additional funds were thus made available to the provider unit to undertake what was acknowledged to be a high risk experimental project. There was a sense among the professionals involved that they had an opportunity to make a difference to the way mental health care would be delivered to the community that they served which would be unlikely to present itself again. There would be no returning to the institution if the outcomes of the home treatment to be offered in West Birmingham were as good as those which had been reported in the USA, Australia, and in Europe. However, staff were equally aware of the enormous burden of responsibility to ensure this project was successful. The dedication and commitment of the people working on the team was remarkable. The Consultant Psychiatrist became available 24 hours a day throughout the initial two year period of the service, and nurses changed their working patterns to include on-call availability, in order to provide round-the-clock community based mental health care.

In 1990, a two year pilot project serving people living in this area of the city demonstrated that it was feasible to treat those with mental health difficulties, including severe psychiatric disorder, using a community based approach as an alternative to hospital admission (Northern Birmingham Mental Health Trust, 1994). As a result of this pilot project, the West Birmingham Home Treatment Team was established to treat and support people in the community experiencing a range of mental health difficulties, including the most severe disorders, and serving a catchment population of 200,000. This catchment area is very deprived and was ranked the fourth most deprived district in England in a study based on the 'Jarman underprivileged area score' (Jarman, 1983). There is high unemployment and a preponderance of multi-occupancy residential units within it and 40 per cent of the population belongs to ethnic minority groups.

How the Home Treatment Team Functions

The team consists of Community Psychiatric Nurses, Mental Health Workers, a Social Worker, the Team Manager and an Administrator. A part-time Consultant Psychiatrist and full time Registrar provides the medical component of the service. Referrals to Home Treatment are made through local Community Mental Health Teams. Once a referral is made two team members visit the person at their normal place of residence to discuss their difficulties and the help that can be offered. Whenever possible immediate family members and carers are involved at this stage. Each person is allocated a 'named worker' who has responsibility for co-ordinating the team's work with the individuals receiving our service.

One of the major findings of the People First survey referred to earlier (Rogers, Pilgrim and Lacey, 1993) was that service users wanted greater involvement in their care planning. Care plans are jointly formulated with service users. Team members have a variety of skills which enable a range of responses to be made in alleviating distress, skills which include expertise in relaxation, massage, cognitive therapy, and individual and family counselling, as well as in social support.

We find a wide variety of needs and problems among our clients. Some of the situations which staff have helped to resolve relate to the following list of commonly encountered issues:

- access to food and basic items;
- shelter;
- shopping;
- cooking;
- legal advice;
- electricity/gas tokens;
- child care;
- dog walking;
- housework;
- loneliness/isolation;
- lack of information;
- more apparently traditional needs in terms of medication and counselling;
- welfare benefits; and
- going to church/mosques/temples and seeing a religious leader.

As an example of the type of individual being referred to the team, the case of an African Caribbean woman in her mid 20s, a mother of two young children, can be considered. She is a lone parent, but with an ex-partner as her main support. She has had a history of admissions to the local psychiatric hospital. We were asked to see her by the Approved Social Worker, who had carried out a Mental Health Act assessment following medical recommendations by two doctors for her to be admitted to hospital again. She was reported to be depressed and suicidal, unable to care for herself or her children. The Social Worker was reluctant to spilt the family unit and asked the team to see her and assess whether or not we would be able to help her. Initially we visited her three times a day for the first few days, spent long periods of time with her, learned about her life history, and offered treatment and support, particularly in terms of practical assistance. She needed assistance with child care both day and night. Her family lived in Bradford, and so were not in a position to help her with the children. Contact was made, with her permission, to seek the help of her ex-partner in caring for the children. The local Social Services department, through the home care team, also provided some assistance with child care, as well as a night-sitter after much discussion with the team manager. A small sum of money was also granted from a local charity which enabled her to purchase a much needed pushchair for the youngest child.

At one stage in her involvement with the team, our client took an overdose of tablets, for which she required medical treatment from the local Accident and Emergency department. The overdose appeared to have been the catalyst towards a deeper therapeutic relationship between her and one member of staff. She disclosed a history of sexual abuse for the first time to professional staff which helped in our understanding of her distress and maximised the assessment of her needs. There were of course difficult clinical decisions to make in order to safely care for this young woman in the community and prevent a further admission to the hospital system which had failed her in the past. The issue of risk assessment and risk management is one which is constantly debated within the team and is central in the working practices of the team. Individual choice, rights, risk to self or others, all had to be managed within a service which was attempting to replace the traditional method of delivering acute mental health care in the area.

Moving from an institutional setting to practice in the community has meant that the team has had to re-examine aspects of their training as mental health workers. They have had to develop skills which are relevant to the practical concerns of the users of the service, along with the more difficult task of changing discriminatory attitudes and behaviour towards black service users. The team tries to avoid coercive interventions; treatment is based on consent and as much as possible on agreement with the service user and his/her relative. Negotiation is stressed with regard to issues such as visiting times and medication. The successful outcome of Home Treatment relies on the team being able to establish 'positive engagement' with the user. This is about building trust, actively listening, encouraging the individual to tell their own story. The shifting of service provision to the patient's home provides a different base from which to make plans and gain understanding of the particular difficulties. It enables the team to understand the context of an individual's current crisis. This means that appropriate responses to the person's needs are made and that there is an avoidance of simply focusing on so-called psychopathology.

Review meetings are held three times a week, where care programmes are evaluated and updated. These meetings are open to the user and his/her relatives. The team continues to be involved with the user until there has been some resolution of the needs that were initially identified and the user has begun to feel more confident in dealing with his or her difficulties. Completion of Home Treatment happens when immediate needs have thus been addressed to a significant extent, and when long term needs have been identified, together with ways of addressing them that have been negotiated with the user, his or her carers and a keyworker from the local Community Mental Health Team.

The West Birmingham Home Treatment Service aims to provide a quite distinct alternative to hospital for people who are in acute distress. The success of the service over the past few years has demonstrated that community based interventions can work and are indeed preferred by the majority of clients. Over the first two years the service was running only 33 (15 per cent) of the 216 people treated by the team required hospital admission. However perhaps the most important effect has been with regard to the quality of intervention achieved. Transfer of resources from the large institutions has often meant the transportation of medical models into the community. In many ways community psychiatry has tended to operate with models that service users and their supporters have been criticising for a number of years. The Home Treatment approach in which the user's own home becomes the focus of intervention tends to challenge the legacy of institutional psychiatry. The social context of the user's distress is highlighted and we believe that more appropriate interventions are delivered. Ultimately there is a shift in the balance of power from providers to users of the service.

The Crisis House

After the service had been operating for several years we developed a plan for a crisis house which could provide sufferers with a break from the domestic situation in which they found themselves. The majority of requests for alternative accommodation had been found to be due to a client (or carer) seeking some relief and/or space from the intense home environment. Such provision was usually required immediately, and for a relatively short space of time. Alternative accommodation was thus being sought in order to offer 'time out' or 'refuge' from a situation causing or contributing to a client's difficulties. Other support, notably meals could often also be required.

Crisis facilities in their various forms constitute a shift towards a comprehensive alternative service but do not generally offer accommodation. This situation applies as much to user led initiatives as to the professional ventures by established statutory agencies, and those which are collaborative in nature. The majority of crisis service comprise teams which usually offer a 24 hour service, but which are unable to provide access to crisis accommodation other than in the local hospital. But the predominant user view is that 'refuge' is needed and that while Home Treatment is the preferable option for many people a choice of sanctuary is still required (see *OpenMind* No. 63). Provision of the latter is seen by some to be a natural extension of developing alternatives to hospital admission and of moving away from categorising an individual's crisis in medical terms. Experience in Home Treatment shows that people in distress both request and value alternative accommodation. The same is also true for families and carers who sometimes require a break from the situation.

Prior to the establishment of the crisis house, meeting this need involved the team in utilising local community resources. The arrangements were dependent on clients having previous connections with an organisation and on vacancies being available, and while possible to make, were found to have inherent difficulties. Some of these related to funding and others to the matching up of client need to the most appropriate shelter setting. When reliance on vacancies is coupled with the mental health dimension, obtaining accommodation becomes a 'hit and miss' affair. If the Home Treatment Team was to have direct access to accommodation 'belonging' to it, then these difficulties could be circumvented. Thus it was that the objectives of (a) offering a (safe space) therapeutic environment when circumstances at home are contributing to the immediate stresses of a clients situation or putting undue stress on carers, and (b) acting to make admission to hospital less likely by providing an alternative shelter, became the principal focus of the team during the period in which planning for a crisis house evolved.

Fortunately a local black-led housing association with a particular interest in mental health issues affecting black people and a history of providing mental health services principally, but not exclusively, to the African-Caribbean community was seeking to expand its range of service provision. The Mental Health Trust entered into a contractual agreement, whereby the housing association would provide a four bedroom house to an agreed specification, and some support staffing. Both clients and the support staff were to have direct access to the Home Treatment Team. So long as clients stayed at the crisis house the full support of the Home Treatment Team would be available both to them and to the staff at the house, 24 hours a day. It was thus to serve as a 'home from home' giving 'time out' to individuals and their families/carers.

The crisis house facility became a victim of its success and there were many occasions when respite was needed by a client but the house was full. A number of circumstances contributed to the situation, but most notably was when the client had a longer term need such as finding a suitable home. Living in the inner city of Birmingham, people struggle with major social inequalities and the sense of hopelessness associated with such factors as long term unemployment, poverty, homelessness, discrimination, social isolation and lack of support with child care. These factors clearly work adversely against the mental health of black men and women and are easily visible to members of the Home Treatment Team. Often this created a sense of impotence amongst the staff group which had to be discussed and worked through before the staff member could be effective in his or her role.

Improving the Service to Black and Ethnic Minority Communities

During 1995, in keeping with our desire to offer better services to those who had been less well served in the past by the local psychiatric hospital, the team held a series of facilitated group discussions, leading on to two whole day sessions devoted to the subject of 'improving the service to black and minority service users'. The sessions brought up issues which it is likely that crisis service and home treatment managers, staff and users are grappling with in most inner city areas. It was within these sessions that some of the key points for this chapter, about race and culture in psychiatric domiciliary services came to the fore. I think it is important that these issues are debated if services are to continue to work towards an anti-discriminatory position.

A major issue which emerged was the expectation of staff to work with the dominant (white) values of the organisation whilst delivering a service to a predominantly black community. Services based on eurocentric philosophies and ideologies have failed the community in the past. The body of knowledge on which the mental health assessment is based usually fails to recognise the positive ideologies about life, the socially constructive beliefs and values that come from African-Caribbean and Asian worlds.

Another issue that came up was that of black staff being asked to work with black clients. It was perceived by some that there was a general unwillingness to work with black clients. It can clearly be seen that home treatment teams working in inner city areas such as ours are always having to guard against an unwritten 'black-on-black' policy coming into place. Such a policy would of course be discriminatory. This would be for several reasons. Firstly, it would mean that black staff would not be given the scope to develop either the range of their abilities or the specialist skills which they might wish to practice. They would be allocated to clients on the basis of assumed greater understanding by virtue of their having the same skin colour as the client, rather than the basis of their knowledge and capacity to respond to the particular situation that the person to whom they were offering assistance might be in. Secondly, it would run the risk of establishing a 'service within a service' for black people. This would be discriminatory because clients would not then necessarily have the opportunity to benefit from the entire range of skills available within the team. Thirdly, it would add to the stigma of black clients, particularly in relation to their often being perceived, in the case of young black males, as violent or dangerous.

Much of the discussion on the issue of race and culture reinforce the point made by Leiba, in chapter 2 of this book, that it is the duty of white workers to find out about culture, rather than to pass the buck on to black workers.

Team members indicated that they would like to obtain more knowledge about the cultural aspects of mental health among Asian women over the age of 40. Similarly they wanted to be able to distinguish more closely the specific culturally related needs of older black people in general. They also wanted to gain knowledge and skills in black and transcultural counselling.

In all of this discussion of culture there is often an assumption that black cultures are necessarily quite different from white ones. Torkington (1991, p. 123) argues that the majority of African-Caribbean people in contact with mental health services are from two, three or even four generations of people living in Britain. 'Their culture is now British and any mental illness among this group should be assessed within the context of the British culture of which they are a part and within which they have to cope with problems of daily living'. Clearly when one remembers that in a city such as Birmingham, most young black people have been brought up in a multicultural UK environment, the boundaries between black and white cultures are less clear cut. As Gilroy suggests in his well known (1984) book *There Ain't no Black in the Union Jack*, black youth and white youth have more in common than not, in terms of social activities and lifestyles. Their social life in cities such as Birmingham is thus not one which is generally either exclusively white or black. The increasing numbers of so called 'mixed race' children in the big cities is a clear illustration of the difficulty created for mental health staff if they work with fixed ideas about e.g. ganga smoking, reggae loving, Rastafarian black youth culture. As Tizard and Phoenix (1993) found in their interviews of mixed race youth in London, such young people tend to regard themselves as primarily Londoners rather than English, or Jamaican, or any other cultural category.

It is perhaps because culture is a more comfortable and acceptable topic than racism and discrimination, that there may often be an over emphasis on cultural differences in relation to current UK mental health services. Cultural differences are important in many instances, for instance for the Chinese and Vietnamese in our city, or for Asian communities, but they are not so important in others.

A feature of the home treatment service is that, as has been noted, it places the client's environment and domestic circumstances at the centre of the assessment and intervention offered. 'In this first contact – often in the intense atmospheres of an acute crisis', as Querido (1969) puts it, 'a picture is unfolded which, I am convinced, never can be obtained in any other way'. When a person is admitted to hospital, the staff who assess and care for him or her do not have to respond to or take into account the domestic situation and the tensions between the people who are participating in it, except at one remove, as these things are reported by third parties to have the status of important psychiatric facts. These home tensions are difficult to assess and respond to, since the treatment service is attempting to address a social network rather than the person in isolation. Inevitably such an objective means that workers always wish to, and must be able to bring as a team, a wide variety of skills to the situation, skills such as family therapy or group counselling which they do not all possess individually. Thus staff attending the sessions on improving the service felt there was a pressure on them to know everything. Without the array of skills to face the intensity of the home situations, particularly the transcultural assessment and support skills, they lacked confidence.

This problem is perhaps linked to our preferred way of working, through a named worker system. Whilst staff wanted to develop the kind of skills that would enable them to offer a wide variety of appropriate responses, naturally they could not be all things to all clients. The importance of a more honest acknowledgement of lack of specialist skills was something that came out of this discussion. But for staff to continue to be less defensive about their lack of specialist skills they would require support from managers for their openness. This problem is not to be underestimated in nursing, where there is a well known tendency for staff not to speak out of turn on account of being branded troublemakers (Salvage, 1985).

Another feature of the home treatment service is that as staff duties are primarily off-site and consist of visiting clients, and as the staff shift pattern in the NHS means that there are rarely opportunities for team meetings which all can attend, communication issues inevitably come to the fore. Staff become isolated to varying degrees and this can lead to feelings of being unsupported by peers and managers. This came out in the sessions on improving services. Staff felt that team work issues were not being given enough attention. Some expressed the need to be more involved in decision making about the service, and for their to be a collaborative determination of service priorities between management, staff and users. A forum might be created for this purpose, it was suggested. Linked to these concerns was the identification of some problems with the medical staff. It was felt that medics did not always have sufficient knowledge of social and cultural issues, that the transportation of the medical model from the local psychiatric hospital was a limitation to the team's development, and that some psychiatrists tended to see the efforts of other staff to take initiatives in terms of threats to their own power base. Psychiatrists, some felt, too often arrogated to themselves the position of the expert. When the peripatetic nature of the team duties is considered in the light of these perceptions of management and clinical direction, it is easy to see that it is difficult for a home treatment service to widen opportunities for its members to be involved with decision making, however democratic the administrators try to be.

This issue highlights what is perhaps a rather crucial problem for community care services in general, that with clients being assessed and treated at home they lack any input into the general running of the services which they are receiving. Of course they are deeply involved in their own care plans, but not in the decision about the broad range of approaches to their needs and the kind of service response to them, that might be available. In hospital, participation of this kind is always more to the fore since patients are able to gather with others receiving services. They can also much more easily communicate their views about services direct to managers and clinical managers, whether in the ward meetings and groups or by personal one to one communication. So it is not surprising that staff felt that the lines of communication were not strong enough between managers, the team and the clients. This is another ongoing problem for home treatment managers to address. As I discuss below, we are making progress in North Birmingham, in respect of this issue, by carrying out satisfaction surveys, and by having regular discussions and meetings with key local black organisations, so that the black voice is listened to and taken account of.

The key element in responding to these issues and in making the service more responsive to minority ethnic clients, indeed to all clients, is to give, adequate support and supervision to team staff. In our sessions on how we might improve service some staff highlighted an unsupported atmosphere with an unstructured use of supervision, as they perceived it. They wanted more constructive and regular feedback, with a commitment to personal supervision. In this way they felt that they would be more listened to and valued. Clinical supervision focusing on professional growth and development, clinical practice issues, challenge and support, following an agreed format, was thus established in the team. Professional management is provided through the line management arrangements of the Mental Health Trust and staff have become more pro-active about their own learning. Of course this meant allocating staff time away from direct care and the support of the senior management was necessary for the system to succeed.

Another factor in the issues raised on how we might become more ethnosensitive involved the team adopting a multifaceted approach in order to turn the service around. Developing a philosophy or mission statement to which all team members subscribe was instrumental in the process. In our service the mission was to provide a flexible, accessible and acceptable service to the community, where the overall needs of the individual would be recognised, rather than just the medical needs being emphasised. The provision of basic needs such as electricity or gas tokens in some cases took priority over medication. Medication is not seen as the main and only source of treatment, but as one option, not the sole basis for support.

Shifting service provision from the hospital to the client's home provides a different base from which plans can be made and a broader understanding reached in terms of individuals difficulties. The avoidance of diagnostic labels with their racial bias that can hinder a worker's potential in supporting clients in a way that is empowering rather than fostering dependence became paramount. Staff became skilled in establishing 'positive engagement' with individuals and their families concerning the basic needs of daily living. This is about building trust, actively listening and allowing clients to tell their own stories. Crisis and social systems intervention became a routine part of the staff daily work. Where family relationships had broken down and contacts lost, with the client's permission team members, usually the 'named worker', would approach the individual family member or encourage the client to make that contact. Where family problems are relevant to both the symptoms of the client and the referral for treatment, these are focused on during our interventions, anti-racist attitudes and cultural sensitivity is therefore fundamental in all staff.

Because eurocentric expertise was well entrenched within the staff team – embodying, for instance, assumptions about the individual's sole responsibility for his or her actions and Judaeo-Christian values of independence, we established regular training forums where staff shared aspects of their own culture with their colleagues. Very often this would involve, as a warm up to the discussion of cultural issues, staff sharing food at the start of the session. It was in one such session that I first tasted the Irish dish of boiled cabbage and bacon! Professional trainers, relatives, carers and clients all contributed to our multicultural and anti-discriminatory training. Joint working within the staff group and closer working relationships with local black community groups and service providers contributed to the reworking of some of our policies on improving services to black and minority service users.

Significant attempts were made to reflect the local community in the composition of the staff group with 50 per cent being either from an Asian or an African-Caribbean background. Community Psychiatric Nurses make up the largest group within the team. Staff have been employed for their professional as well as their bilingual skills. Another strategy used to address some of the communication problems associated with shift work has been to change the pattern to allow for all staff to meet fortnightly and to make attendance to staff meetings mandatory. As mentioned above, service users opinions were regularly canvassed through satisfaction surveys and meetings with key black organisations were held in order that the black voice in the decision making process of the team was heard and taken account of. These links have proved essential to the success of the home treatment service.

Many black people entering the mental health system already feel oppressed by their experience of racial discrimination, unemployment, poor housing and so on. They feel they have little control over their own lives and often regard psychiatric intervention as another problem rather than a solution. Simply treating mental ill health with medication alone, as in the experience of many black people, only exacerbates the situation, particularly as many in the black community feel that mental ill health is not the direct cause of their condition. To attempt to assess mental state without addressing fundamental needs only represents a response consisting of short term solutions. The home treatment service places emphasis on assessing the range of needs of the individual client which reflect the social circumstances in which they are living. The assessment thus has to be adaptable and flexible, rather than being of the traditional state-of-mental-health and information from relatives type. This flexibility, in turn, leads to local community resources, both statutory and non statutory, being used as part of the solution wherever possible. Ultimately it is the engagement of individuals, their families, the wider community and other agencies, coupled with special training for all staff working with black and minority ethnic people, on race and mental health, that is likely to bring about a successful outcome for home treatment services. The challenge for Trusts as providers is to avoid the wholesale transportation of eurocentric practice as they move towards alternative interventions such as home treatment services.

References

Audit Commission (1994), *Finding a Place*, HMSO, London.

Department of Health (1992), *Services for people from Black and Ethnic Minority groups: Issues of Race and Culture, in Review of Health and Social Services for Mentally Disordered Offenders and Others requiring similar Services*, HMSO, London.

Francis, E., David, J., Johnson, N. and Sashidharan, S.P. (1993), 'Black People and Psychiatry in the UK', in Clarke, P., Harrison, M., Patel, K., Shah, M. and Zack-Williams, T. (eds), *Improving Mental Health Practice*, Central Council for Education and Training in Social Work, Leeds.

Gilroy, P. (1987), *There Ain't no Black in the Union Jack*, Hutchinson, London.

Heller, T., Reynolds, J., Gomm, R. and Muston, R. (1996), *Mental Health Matters: A Reader*, Open University/Macmillan, Basingstoke.

Jarman, B. (1983), 'Identification of under-privileged areas', *British Medical Journal*, Vol. 286, pp. 1705–8.

Littlewood, R. and Lipsedge, M. (1981), 'Some social and phenomenological characteristics of psychotic immigrants', *Psychological Medicine*, Vol. 11, pp. 289–302.

Littlewood, R. and Lipsedge, M. (1982), *Aliens and alienists: ethnic minorities and psychiatry*, Penguin, Harmondsworth.

Morgan, S. (1993), *Community Mental Health: Practical Approaches to long term problems*, Chapman and Hall, London.

Northern Birmingham Mental Health Trust (1995), *Annual Report*.

Querido, A. (1969), 'The Shaping of Community Mental Health Care', *British Journal of Psychiatry*, Vol. 114, pp. 293–302.

Rogers, A., Pilgrim, D. and Lacey, R. (1993), *Experiencing Psychiatry: User's Views of Services*, Macmillan, Basingstoke.

Salvage, A. (1985), *The Politics of Nursing*, Heinemann, London.

Tizard, B. and Phoenix, A. (1993), *Black, White or Mixed Race? Race and Racism in the Lives of Young People of Mixed Parentage*, Routledge, London.

Torkington, P. (1991), *Black Health – A Political Issue*, Catholic Association for Racial Justice, London.

7 The Effectiveness of Crisis Services

KEVIN HOGAN AND SARAH ORME

Introduction

This chapter will begin by outlining the context within which crisis services are evaluated. It will describe how the literature suggests effectiveness of services should be measured. A description of frequently cited research studies is included to form a base from which to critique methods of evaluation used so far. Finally, the authors suggest how research can move on to take more account of the expressed needs of mental health service users.

Background

In the light of permanent competition for resources in all publicly funded health systems, providers need to demonstrate to purchasers how their money is spent and what it achieves; particularly in order to justify new services. Consequently, services need to be evaluated and measured in a robust and repeatable manner. This chapter discusses the role of cost and cost effectiveness evaluations in the development of mental health crisis services. The present work is based on a review of the evaluation literature, data from our work in progress – a survey of the national position with regards to the development of such services – and a single evaluation case study already reported elsewhere (Hogan et al., 1997b; Hogan and Orme, 1997).

What is Effectiveness?

It is important at the outset to clarify what it is that we mean by the measurement of costs, cost effectiveness and outcomes, as these ideas lie at the heart of this review. The definition of what constitutes costs and the measurement of such in health settings is complicated (McCrone and Weich, 1996) but we propose to limit our discussion of costs to the measurement of direct, indirect and hidden costs in service evaluations. According to McCrone and Weich, direct costs are those due to contact with specialist mental health services and indirect costs refer to those caused through service contacts not primarily part of the mental health care system. Hidden costs are considered to be those resulting in a loss of production, due to mental health problems, that are not readily observable. McCrone and Weich suggest the burden experienced by families, lost employment for users, friends and family, lost leisure time for friends and family, and users' travelling and waiting times are all hidden costs. We suggest, however, that these costs are observable and real to the users of services and their informal carers. They are also quantifiable in terms of hours/days of lost employment or waiting times, and these losses can be expressed in monetary terms if need be. That is, we do not consider the costs described as hidden by McCrone and Weich actually to be so.

We would like to suggest that still other costs are more deeply embedded, and thus require a deal of effort to detect, within the experience of mental ill-health. For example, the burden of care may lead a carer to contact services for help with stress. In the specific case of crisis services, the carer may be the one seeking help although the known client may still be the one treated (Hogan et al., 1997a). An increase in prescriptions for sleeping tablets or tranquillisers for carers, or increased numbers of General Practitioner contacts, are both hidden costs. Finally, as costs are calculated once a person becomes a 'case', traditional cost measurement will miss the increased contacts users make with services in the lead up to their crisis. To summarise, we suggest hidden costs are more hidden than previously documented, but that they need to be revealed and given consideration, in order to generate as accurate a picture as possible of the effects of mental ill health and mental health service interventions.

In our discussion of cost effectiveness we will follow the usage of Bowling (1997, p. 83) who defined cost effectiveness as 'the ratio of the net change in health care costs to the net change in health outcomes'. In order to measure effectiveness in line with the previous definition a measure of health outcomes is required; in short studies should employ a standardised instrument, or instruments, that measures the consequences of the intervention(s) on the clinical status of service users.

Finally, Yuen (1994) makes a clear distinction between the measurement of the quality of mental health services (i.e., the achievement of outcomes in terms of programme objectives) and their effectiveness (i.e., whether clients benefit from the service provided). This distinction needs to be borne in mind in light of Yuen's further assertion that the two, quality and effectiveness, are used synonymously. For example, services are frequently reported to be effective if they have reduced the number of inpatient hospital admissions (a programme objective) regardless of whether this intervention has helped clients. In the following discussion we use the term effectiveness, although some research referred to is more likely to have measured quality in line with Yuen's terminology. Clearly, this is a distinction worth making, particularly in the light of an institutional commitment to take account of users' views.

Literature on Crisis Services

We have undertaken a review of UK studies of the last ten years that examine crisis services, however constituted, and which report positive benefits of the intervention. The purpose of this latter criterion is to allow us to examine the evidence for the considerable growth in crisis intervention work and services in the last ten years (Value for Money Unit, 1997). North American studies were excluded on the grounds that the definition of a crisis service, whilst broad in the UK context, is stretched beyond the bounds of utility in these accounts. The North American definition includes hospitalisation as a valid therapeutic response whereas the philosophy of crisis services in the UK generally supports a view of them as alternatives to hospital admission.

Previous Evaluations of Crisis Services

The four case studies described below do not represent the results of a systematic review. Instead they were found through searches of electronic databases (Cinahl, Medline, PsycLit, Bath Information Data Service) using the search terns 'crisis' and 'effectiveness'. All four are cited elsewhere in the literature as examples of studies that exhibit the effectiveness of crisis services (Beer et al., 1995; Ratna, 1996), and make an attempt to consider the effects of services on clients' symptoms and the financial or social costs of services. The case studies are summarised in Table 7.1 at the end of the chapter.

Case Study 1. Huddersfield West Crisis Intervention Team (CIT) (Punukollu 1991)

Punukollu reported the outcomes of an evaluation of the six-month pilot project

(1 January to 30 June 1986) of the Huddersfield CIT. Clients were offered multidisciplinary care and followed intensively in their own homes and in the community, which involved clients' carers, family and neighbours. During the six-month pilot, 54 clients were offered crisis intervention. The first 15 of these clients approached who met the inclusion criteria (no organic brain disorder, no substance/alcohol abuse, no psychiatric admission within the previous two years) and agreed to participate, were examined in detail.

Punukollu calculated the costs of traditional treatment on the basis of a six-month in-patient stay at 1984 and 1985 charges. In-patient bed and out-patient costs post-discharge were compared to crisis costs consisting of travelling times, expenses and the professional time spent with clients. This process resulted in crisis intervention costs being found to be six times less than traditional hospital treatment. No test statistic was reported to indicate the significance of this difference.

Relative's burden was measured using the Social Behavioural Assessment Schedule (SBAS), a measure of subjective and objective burden. This measure was completed within a week of clients' first interviews and within two months of discharge. Burden was reported to improve on all subscales between time one and time two; a p-value is reported but not the statistical test performed that generated this value.

Client functioning was measured with the General Health Questionnaire (GHQ)-30 within a week of assessment by the CIT and within two months of discharge. A significant difference between baseline and discharge scores was reported using a Mann-Whitney U statistic: crisis intervention was reported to have resulted in an improvement in symptoms. No control condition was included.

Admission figures for the four consultant psychiatrists in the Huddersfield district were compared over three six-month periods (January–June 1984, 1985 and 1986). The non-crisis consultant admissions increased steadily over each three month period whereas the crisis consultant admissions showed a slow decrease. The average length of stay of the crisis consultant's admissions was reported to decrease gradually from 1984 to 1986, from 23 to 17 days and was suggested to be due to the crisis intervention project. Again, a p-value but no test statistic is reported. In the crisis intervention area, first admission figures reduced from around 50 per cent in 1984 to 20 per cent in 1986. Eleven of the 54 clients offered crisis intervention therapy were admitted (20 per cent). Reasons for their admission were not provided, nor was it explained whether hospital admission was an acceptable component of crisis intervention or if these clients were considered as crisis intervention failures.

Case Study 2. The Daily Living Programme (DLP) (Muijen et al., 1992; Marks et al., 1994; Knapp et al., 1994)

The Daily Living Programme (DLP: Muijen et al., 1992; Knapp et al., 1994; Marks et al., 1994) was developed to provide a comprehensive alternative service for clients who would otherwise be facing emergency admissions to the Bethlem-Maudsley Hospital. It offered a long-term approach, cared for clients in their own homes and included a crisis intervention component. It offered multidisciplinary, 24-hour care, seven days a week in the form of a walk in clinic at the Maudsley and telephone access at night. Treatment was provided at the place of breakdown and admissions prevented if possible. A needs-based, case management approach with key workers was provided.

Marks et al. (1994) and Knapp et al. (1994) reported the results of a randomised controlled study in which clients facing admission (over 26 months) were randomised to DLP or standard inpatient and outpatient care and followed for 18 months. To be included clients had to be aged 17-64, have no primary addiction or organic brain syndrome, have a serious mental illness requiring urgent hospital admission, not be pregnant and live in the catchment area of the hospital. Before entry clients and their carers were asked if they agreed to either treatment modality.

Knapp et al. reported that the DLP was a cost effective alternative to standard treatment. They included long-run marginal costs (see Bowling, 1997 for a definition) and compared the (direct) service and accommodation costs incurred by the DLP with (direct) costs incurred by standard inpatient care groups. Total service and accommodation costs were found to be less in the DLP treatment group at four, 11 and 20 months after entry into the study. Knapp et al. concluded that the DLP was less expensive than standard client care over 20 months, in relation to direct costs. When taken together with the findings of Marks et al. (1994) of greater improvements of clients' symptoms in the DLP group (see below), the DLP can be seen to have provided a cost effective alternative to standard psychiatric care.

In relation to indirect costs, Knapp et al. also examined lost employment of clients , with similar proportions of clients in both DLP and hospital groups in full time work at baseline and at 20 months. There was no evidence to suggest a differential effect of the DLP on employment costs, but actual figures were not reported. Hidden family and informal care costs were also considered, however, lack of concentrated intervention with clients' families did not allow for the enumeration of these costs. Informal costs considered included accommodation, time spent by carers at home with the client and time spent by the client with friends and relatives; no differences were found in the amount of these behaviours in the two groups.

Ratings of client symptoms using the Global Assessment Scale (GAS), Present State Examination (PSE), Brief Psychiatric Rating Scale (BPRS) and Social Adjustment Scale (SAS) were made within 72 hours of entry into the study and, along with ratings of client and patient satisfaction, at four, 11 and 20 months (Marks et al., 1994). Details were available for 92 DLP and 97 control clients and at baseline the two groups did not differ significantly on demographics, PSE diagnoses or magnitude of psychopathology. The DLP group also had fewer previous admissions to the Bethlem-Maudsley and fewer clients on a Mental Health Act section. Both DLP and control clients improved on all clinical measures by month four, and again at 11 and 20 months. For the groups as a whole the DLP treatment was seen to be slightly superior in improving client functioning. However, superiority of outcomes varied at each time period. For example the BPRS showed greater improvements in the DLP group only at 20 months ($p=0.03$), the PSE total score is reported as having favoured the DLP group again only at 20 months ($p=0.09$), GAS scores were reported to be significantly different at four months ($p=0.08$) and 20 months ($p=0.09$). Clients and relatives were satisfied with both forms of care, but more so with DLP care for both clients ($p<0.009$ at 11 and 20 months) and relatives ($p<0.11$ at four, $p<0.001$ at 11 and $p<0.05$ at 20 months).

Marks et al. reported that only 12 per cent of DLP clients did not have admissions over the 20 months; all of the standard group were admitted. Length of in-patient stay was reported to be 80 per cent less in the DLP group; an average admission of 18 days in the DLP group compared to 76 in the controls over the 18 month study period. However, during the course of the study, responsibility for DLP clients on in-patient wards transferred from the DLP team to ward staff. After this time, lengths of stay in the DLP group trebled.

Case Study 3. Sparkbrook Home Treatment Service (Dean and Gadd, 1990; Dean et al., 1993)

Dean and Gadd (1990) and Dean et al. (1993) have both evaluated the Sparkbrook home-treatment programme. The service is an inner city (Birmingham), 24-hour, multidisciplinary service targeted at seriously ill people (those threatening suicide, displaying aggressive behaviour or psychotic) who would normally be admitted to hospital. The home treatment team is housed in a multidisciplinary resource centre that offers support for relatives and a drop-in centre for clients. Referrals are accepted from any agency, including self-referrals, clients are treated intensively at home and followed-up at discharge through out-patient clinics run from the resource centre.

Dean et al. (1993) compared the outcomes for clients facing admission to hospital in Sparkbrook and in Small Heath – another area of Birmingham of similar ethnic make-up and deprived status that offered acute care at an in-patient unit in a large psychiatric hospital. Clients suffering acute episodes of illness and likely to be admitted (persons at risk to self or others and in need of 24-hour speciality services) were followed over a 13 month period. Clients and their carers gave their consent to be interviewed.

In the Dean et al. (1993) study, carers were interviewed using the Social Behavioural Assessment Schedule, the GHQ and burden and satisfaction self-rated questionnaires (developed by Hoult et al., 1984) on three occasions (within ten days of patient admission, at one month and one year). Similar scores on all subscales of the SBAS were found in both groups at all assessment times. However, the Sparkbrook carers exhibited less objective burden at baseline, and at one month they experienced less distress due to clients' social performance than Small Heath carers. There were no differences between the groups of carers of GHQ scores initially, at one month or at one year. More Sparkbrook relatives were very satisfied and less dissatisfied then in the Small Heath group with the care the clients received and the support and information they received.

In terms of outcome measures for clients of the home treatment service and of the hospital, these were assessed with (a) the Present State Examination within three days of admission and 12 months after entry into the study; (b) the Morningside rehabilitation scale at initial assessment and once a week for six weeks; and (c) the Comprehensive Psychiatric Rating Scale weekly for four weeks (Dean et al., 1993). The initial scores on the PSE were the same in both groups: both groups improved and there were no differences in the scores of the two groups after a year. There were no differences in scores on the Morningside rehabilitation scores apart from in week two when the Sparkbrook group exhibited significantly better functioning.

Dean and Gadd's (1990) study also reported on a comparison of home and hospital treated clients. Retrospectively, case notes were compared for all clients aged 16-65 in the Sparkbrook area who were received into acute mental health care over a two year period (1 October 1987 to 30 September 1989), whether they had been treated at home or in hospital. No exclusion criteria were employed. Clients admitted to other hospitals in the district under another psychiatrist were also included.

Characteristics of clients managed under home treatment were compared to clients admitted at any time during their treatment. Dean and Gadd (1990) reported the results for the second year of the operation of the service when a 24-hour on-call service had been introduced. During this year 65 episodes (56 clients) were treated at home and 34 episodes (24 clients) in hospital. Of those admitted in the second year, 12 (35 per cent) were assessed as unsuitable for home treatment, 15 (44 per cent) were admitted without assessment and seven (21 per cent) were admitted after a period of home treatment. Average bed occupancy was reported to have reduced over the period of this second year's operation from ten to five days.

In Dean et al.'s (1993) comparative study of treatment in Sparkbrook and Small Heath, 69 clients in Sparkbrook and 55 in Small Health were eligible for inclusion. Of the home treatment group 24 (35 per cent) were admitted initially and 45 (65 per cent) received all their care at home or the resource centre. All of the Small Heath group were admitted. Hospital admission was utilised by the home treatment team if deemed necessary, but exhibited lower lengths of stay at first admission (8.3 days vs. 58.7) and throughout the following year (20.6 days vs. 67.9) than in the Small Health area.

Case Study 4. Wimbledon, Mitcham and Wandsworth (Burns et al., 1993a; 1993b)

Two sector teams in each of the London areas of Wimbledon, Mitcham and Wandsworth were amalgamated and then continued to practice either in their normal way or in an experimental way based on the Dingleton (Jones, 1987) model of community based psychiatric care. This operated with home-based, joint assessments of clients, multidisciplinary team working, regular meetings and a philosophy of crisis intervention (Burns et al., 1993a). All clients referred to the teams between October 1987 and October 1989 were randomised on referral by a research secretary to receive either standard care or the experimental community care. Inclusion criteria were that clients were aged 18–74, lived in the catchment area, had not received treatment in the last 12 months and could be interviewed in English.

In order to assess direct costs, clients case notes were used to identify in-patient and out-patient service use. General Practitioner and social work contacts were attached to client case notes and any other psychiatric contacts that were evident from case notes costed (Burns et al., 1993b). A similar proportion of clients in both groups visited their GPs during the course of the study and averaged a similar number of visits. General Practitioner unit costs for psychiatric consultations were based on the National Morbidity Study (Croft-Jeffreys and Wilkinson, 1989). More control than experimental clients used social work contacts in a greater number, but these costs were not included. It was suggested that inclusion of these would only have increased the costs of care in the control group.

Unit costs were available for the year 1986/7 at both regional and national levels, and were calculated for 1987/8 by adjusting the 1986/7 figures in terms of inflation at 8.3 per cent. Equal unit costs were used for outpatient appointments and home visits. Labour costs calculated in terms of staff grades and time (including travel costs) were equal. Overhead costs for home visits were not available, but estimated to be less than the 40 per cent of the overheads for outpatient attendances.

Costs of services within the catchment area alone (routine costs) were identified separately from costs of services available at regional level. These were then compared between the two groups. In both cases the experimental group exhibited lower mean treatment costs than the control group. Calculations taking into account the higher number of psychotic clients in the control group, and those that removed clients with organic brain disorder or substance misuse problems, also showed the experimental group to cost less. Burns et al. (1993b) suggested that, as these cost savings were exhibited without additional training of staff or spending on resources, improvements in care can be achieved through the improved use of resources already present in the community.

Income and employment costs were also identified and measured in this study through a questionnaire. There were no apparent differences between the experimental and control group in terms of these, but no elaboration of the lack of any difference in these costs was offered by the authors.

Family burden was also measured by informants reporting whether they experienced no limitations or mild problems on a number of variables. Family burden was reported to be low in both groups and similar in each of them. Eleven carers were considered to experience considerable burden, six in the experimental and five in the control group.

In terms of outcomes for clients of the Dingleton model and comparison group, these were assessed by a researcher within two weeks of referral and again at six weeks, six months and 12 months using a range of assessments including: the Present State Examination (PSE); Brief Psychiatric Rating Scale (BPRS); Social Functioning Schedule (SFS); a consumer satisfaction scale; a clinical interview; the Family Burden Scale; key informants' (carer/family member) ratings of clients' symptoms; and key informants' and clients' satisfaction scales (Burns et al., 1993a). Along with these assessment schedules, demographic information and a social history for each client was recorded.

No demographic or history differences were found at baseline assessment between the two groups, except clients with a PSE CATEGO-defined psychotic rating numbered more in the control group. Clients in both groups improved in the psychiatric and social functioning over the study period (improvements in clinical interview and BPRS at six weeks, and PSE score at 12 months), however no differences in improvements were found between the groups at any assessment point. There were also no differences in informants' ratings of clients' social functioning in the two groups at any time. Satisfaction was expressed by consumers for both services, with no preference for either service.

Use of out-patient care was similar in the two groups in terms of the average number of contacts in each group although the experimental group received a longer mean total time of staff contact than the control group. Fewer experimental clients than control clients were admitted during the study period, and experimental clients had shorter lengths of in-patient stays than the control group. There were also fewer re-admissions in the experimental group. As the achievement of reductions in hospital care was not within the remit of the experimental teams, Burns et al. (1993b) suggested that the experimental team helped clients in a way less disruptive to their own and their families' lives.

Critique

Before continuing with a critique of the evaluation of crisis services, it must be noted that only one of the services described above is still operating. The Huddersfield West CIT did not survive the sectorisation of Huddersfield and stopped operating five years ago. The DLP ceased operating four years ago. The community-based service piloted by Burns et al. ceased operating due to a change in emphasis of services to that of offering intensive outreach for known clients (Burns, 1997). Only the Sparkbrook home treatment service is known to be still operating.

It is not intended to critique the studies included here individually, but rather to use these as a starting block from which to question such studies as a model for evaluation of crisis services as a whole. Uchtenhagen (1986) stated that the different methods and different sources of data applied to evaluate different organisational structures, and constant changes within services themselves, all make it very difficult to draw conclusions from studies or determine what variables are responsible for findings. In other words evaluation studies often cannot account for findings adequately. This may be due, firstly, to inadequate experimental design. For example, no control group is identified at the outset of research (e.g., Punukollu, 1991) rather, retrospective opportunistic comparisons are used to generate findings (e.g., Dean and Gadd, 1990; Kwakwa, 1995). This may result in arbitrary before and after comparisons that do not compare like with like. This also reflects our belief that many evaluations are of neither experimental nor quasi-experimental design. Rather they are empirical studies in that they collect data, but from which no firm conclusions can be drawn. There is no testing of theory nor the development of an evidential base from which to develop theory. We suggest further that much of the crisis service evaluation work we have come across has no theoretical basis. There is no clear definition for what researchers consider a crisis to be and no explanation given for what the service evaluated aims to achieve. This in turn makes it most difficult to evaluate effectiveness in the sense proposed by Yuen (1994).

Secondly, limited space for the reporting of findings may limit the explanation of them. In many evaluations that suggest a service has had a positive impact, alternative explanations for findings are not put forward or discussed. For example, the reduction in admissions in the local hospital following the introduction of a crisis service is suggested to be due to the service enabling people to remain out of hospital, not that GPs are referring their clients to the Social Services Emergency Duty Team who admit clients to a different hospital. Observed changes are accounted for in terms of the operation of the service of interest only, without consideration of the wider mental health service provision.

The point here is not to suggest that services are not effective, but that researchers do not always account for all possible explanations. The first six months operation of the crisis service we evaluated did not result in any changes in hospital admissions. It could, therefore, have been suggested that the service was not fulfilling its goals. However, when we asked the Trust operating the in-patient unit if they could suggest why no changes had taken place, they replied that the in-patient unit was always full (Hogan et al., 1997b). Indeed, in one case a referral to the crisis service had been used to support a client while they waited for an inpatient bed to become free, very much contrary to the alternative to admission remit the service operated under. Such was the demand for beds in the area that any beds that had become free due to the operation of the crisis service would have been filled straight away from other sources. The question to be answered by researchers then is whether the presence of a crisis service accounts for research findings, or the operation of other services not discussed?

Related to the explanation of findings is what results actually mean. In some cases data are not subject to statistical analysis. This is more often the case with in-service evaluations, for example, where raw figures for in-patient admissions may be compared and a lower figure in year two accounted for by the crisis service. In some cases half a statistic is reported, for example, Punukollu (1991) reported p-values without the corresponding test-statistic. Still, in other cases, questions remain about the statistical techniques employed to identify the significant effects of treatments. Suffice it to say, again, that we do not suggest these services are ineffective, but that before conclusions can be drawn about the effectiveness of services, a fuller account of findings needs to be provided in some cases. Causality is neither proven nor adequately discussed.

Cost effectiveness as defined by Bowling (1997) requires that differences in the cost of services are related to improvements in client conditions. Hence the need for standardised measures of clients symptoms that can be used to calculate the degree of improvement per pound spent. In the examples outlined above, all evaluations reported the use of standardised instruments. However, in those that attempted to measure cost effectiveness, none linked improvements in symptoms (if any were found) to cost savings.

It is not enough to say that because a community-based crisis service is £100,000 less expensive than in-patient admissions (over the same period of time treating the same number of clients) that it is cost effective. What are the outcomes for clients experiencing both types of service? Let us suppose both improve equally in terms of their symptoms as measured by a standardised instrument. However, where are clients 12 months after their initial service contacts? If the crisis client has re-presented to the crisis service each quarter and the hospital client has had no further need of any psychiatric service, which service is the most cost effective? Secondly, this 'a costs less than b' approach indicates an incomplete consideration of direct, indirect and hidden costs. For example what are the costs born by the client's family? The carer of a community-based client may suffer stress, depression or anxiety as they care for their loved one, whereas the carer of a client in hospital may feel relief at the respite they are given. The consideration of cost effectiveness, therefore, needs to develop to encompass the relative costs of client improvements in different services.

Finally, with regard to costs, we do not feel that what we have referred to as the more 'embedded' among the hidden costs borne by clients, their carers, and statutory and voluntary services, have been adequately addressed in research to date. Researchers tend to only measure direct service costs and easily observable indirect costs. Where hidden costs such as carer stress and support seeking, carer time spent with the client are addressed, they tend to be only considered at a superficial level and in terms which are difficult to quantify. Additional time and effort would be required to tease out those costs that are more deeply embedded in the experience of mental ill health. This time is often not available to researchers and costs that cannot be enumerated easily are perhaps of less value to the commissioners of research.

Evaluations of crisis services occur in the short term, often in an attempt to consolidate funding or renew contracts. The longevity of services is varied, as can be seen from above, and specifically awarded funds or grants may be temporary. We have come across no replications of research into the effectiveness of crisis services. Moreover, research suggests that services tend to either change and develop or, indeed, cease to operate. The diversity of crisis services available means that findings are not generalisable from one service to another. These factors then determine that the findings from an evaluation are unique and time limited.

To conclude, the evaluation of the effectiveness of crisis services needs to be developed to take account of the issues raised above. There needs to be consideration of the position and role of the crisis service in the context of mental health service provision as a whole. Greater emphasis needs to be placed on what different services can achieve for clients over the long and short term, and the costs of these services to carers, clients and other mental health providers and services that come into contact with the client and/or carer. Ultimately, monetary costs need to be put into the wider perspective so evaluation can focus on the help and healing the different services are able to offer.

What Next?

Having discussed the limitations of the current approaches to crisis service evaluation, what next? The next logical step may be to carry out a randomised controlled trial of crisis services at a national level where the resources for a more thorough approach can be made available. This need arises from the observation that the research skills required to carry out such a project are not widespread in the primary care and community care settings (Mant, 1997) and because the cost of such a study would be prohibitive in the context of the local initiatives which are characteristic in this field. However, it has to be said that such a development may well be premature because of the relatively underdeveloped state of the service philosophy underpinning crisis services and, following on from this, the relatively diverse pattern of service models which characterise the systems that are currently in operation (Value for Money Unit, 1997; Orme and Hogan, forthcoming). Given such a heterogeneous pattern of services the generalisability of the results from a well designed randomised control trial would be seriously limited.

We cannot avoid the conclusion that what has to happen next is that we need to return to the question of what exactly it is that those who propose and operate crisis services are seeking to achieve. In particular, whether or not the development of such services is designed to provide a new form of service that will provide a therapeutic intervention currently missing from areas without such a service; or an alternative and more cost effective model for the arrangement for primary mental health care, or, indeed, some mixture of the two. Finally, and most important perhaps, who are the intended clients for such a service? Are they to be, as is the case in some areas, long term mental health service users or anyone who is suffering a severe crisis with psychological/psychiatric dimensions?

In order to evaluate a service, as a point of reference, we need a clear set of aims and objectives for that service. It is important, therefore, for crisis services to define what they consider to be a crisis. However, our ongoing survey of crisis services and previous review (Hogan et al., 1997b) suggest this is often not normal practice. It is assumed that a crisis is a known quantity. However, services can be seen to offer services to clients suffering greatly different problems.

Jacobs (1983) defined a crisis as 'a turning point that precludes the possibility of life going on as usual' (p. 172). This definition applies to all people whether mental health service users or not. This is important as the work of Caplan (1964), who is often cited as the instigator of the development of crisis intervention services, was directed towards reducing the incidence of mental ill-health in the community before people became service users. It can be seen therefore that the practice of crisis intervention has moved from treating everyone in the community, and the community itself, to treating a distinct group of individuals often with a long and varied psychiatric history (Hogan and Orme, 1997; Hogan et al., 1997a). This is reflected in current government policy that calls for the concentration of services for those clients with enduring and severe mental illness (DoH, 1994) and the consequent reprovision of some mental health services (Burns, 1997). This is not to say that current practice is wrong. Indeed Caplan described his work as not being based on solid research nor a consensus of professional opinion, but this change in emphasis, from primary prevention in the community to secondary and/or tertiary prevention for known clients, needs to be borne in mind. The question arises, are crisis services actually operating as originally envisaged?

Secondly, what is crisis intervention and do current services actually provide it? Renshaw (1989) stated that crisis intervention provides appropriate help quickly to clients with identifiable psychological crises, in order to return them to their pre-crisis level of functioning (Waldron, 1989). However, Hobbs (1984, p. 32) stated that 'there is little consensus, even among practitioners, as to what constitutes crisis intervention. A variety of techniques are applied in a variety of settings to a wide variety of problems, by practitioners with a variety of skills and qualifications, and with a variety of aims'. Again, we have evidence for this through the service specifications we have received from our recent survey (Orme and Hogan, forthcoming).

Thirdly, then, crisis services need to explicitly state what they intend to do, for whom and how they aim to achieve these goals. For example, is the role of the service to reduce in-patient admissions in order to reduce the costs incurred by purchasers? Or is its role to assess, support and treat clients in the community so that users receive the most appropriate care for their crises? In the former case reducing admissions is the *raison d'être*, whereas it may be an inevitable consequence of the latter. With clear service objectives set, the outcomes achieved by a service, and the interventions it offers, can be more readily evaluated. The issue of whether quality or effectiveness has been evaluated will also become increasingly clear.

We suggest, then, that these three aspects of services – what a crisis is, what crisis intervention is considered to be, and the aims of a crisis service – need to be made explicit at the outset of any evaluation. Indeed, services need to make these clear in their service protocols and operational policies in order that purchasers know what they intend to purchase, providers are clear on what they are offering and service users know what care they can expect to receive. It should therefore be possible to measure the effectiveness of services in terms of purchasers', providers' and users' satisfaction with services.

Users' views of services are important as it has been suggested that users are able to inform professionals of which aspects of care resulted in improvements in their conditions (Holloway, 1993). Users, in theory, are therefore able to choose between services in terms of what they feel to be important and suggest to professionals how services may be improved (Spencer, 1996). It is already the case that users' satisfaction is used as evidence to support services (e.g., Kwakwa, 1995; Davis et al., 1985; Parkes, 1992a; 1992b). However, again, it is important to define at the outset of any measurement of satisfaction what it is intended to measure. Ricketts (1992) stated that researchers conceptions of satisfaction differ and this results in both different approaches to measurement and what ultimately is measured. For example, Beech and Norman (1995) measured the quality of services and Sharma et al. (1992) the helpfulness services. However, both are described as studies of client satisfaction.

Differences in language use between users and professionals may disguise differences in their conceptions of a 'crisis service' (Beeforth et al., 1990). Beeforth et al. suggested that professionals see a crisis service as a rapid but still traditional service, whereas clients view crisis services as having a non-medical approach and providing sanctuary without traditional psychiatric interventions. Also of import with the measurement of users' views is whether measures are quantitative or qualitative (Williams, 1995). For example, do they ask about specific aspects of a service, e.g., food or privacy, and only, therefore, measure specific aspects of a service? Or do they ask open-ended questions that may indicate satisfaction or problems with the service as a whole?

Finally, Ruggeri (1996) suggested that some satisfaction measures are inadequate due to a lack of psychometric properties. For example, are measures acceptable to clients – are clients able to understand and complete them (face validity)? Are measures sensitive to changes in satisfaction – can they measure dissatisfaction? Are measures valid – do they actually measure client satisfaction or answer providers' questions (content validity)? Are measures reliable – will similar findings be reported by the same respondent on two different occasions over a short period of time (test-retest reliability)?

It can be seen then that in order to ascertain the views of the mental health service user, more needs to be done than simply writing a questionnaire and distributing it. The intention behind the exercise needs to be made explicit and thorough development and testing of satisfaction measures is required in order that they ask relevant questions in a meaningful way. Indeed, Ruggeri suggests it is time to develop the use of validated measures and carry out comparisons between studies in order to improve existing instruments, rather than to continue to develop and use in-house measures.

A Feasible Approach to Measuring the Cost Effectiveness of Crisis Services

In our view, the continued use of in-house evaluations of effectiveness and users' views is not to be recommended. A national randomised controlled trial of services is both unrealistic and irrelevant due to the diversity of services to be included and lack of an agreed definition of crisis and crisis intervention. An alternative is therefore required. We suggest that the measurement of the effectiveness of crisis services be carried out in two ways. Firstly, the measurement of satisfaction needs to be addressed at the individual client level and secondly, the effectiveness of services needs to be considered in terms of the services aims and goals, and be monitored perhaps through client tracking.

Satisfaction is based on the fulfilment of needs and expectations. By this we mean clients' needs and expectations on entry to a service. The questions we need to ask about such needs and expectations are of the following kind:

- what interventions do clients wish to receive and from whom?
- what do clients want services to do differently from what they are already doing?
- what is the most important thing that is happening now that clients want stopped?

Clients must set their own goals for the outcomes of the service contact and what they want to achieve. Questions to be put here, are, for example:

- does the client want to stop hearing voices?
- does the client want somewhere safe to stay away from their home?

Informal carers also need to be involved and asked what they would like to come out of the service contact. Service evaluators need to know what carers want services to do and to examine, for instance, whether the carer needs some respite? This issue must also be regarded as important. As Yuen (1994) points out, the population served by a mental health service includes clients, carers, mental health workers and the wider community, to name a few. Also little work has been carried out to ascertain whether the mental health services provided are compatible with the needs of all these groups.

We suggest it is important to measure client-defined needs on entry to, and discharge from, a service in order to ascertain whether the service has provided satisfactory care for its clients. As outlined above, provider or purchaser-led questions do not necessarily measure those aspects of care important to users. In-house measures tend to concentrate on those aspects of care that are easily quantifiable, without asking what clients actually wanted, required or thought of the service received.

The before and after approach suggested here will enable providers to identify what clients want when they enter a service and make some attempt to meet these needs. Users' groups have been vocal about aspects of care they feel crisis services should offer, for example 24-hour access to care, service planning based on users' needs (Cobb, 1995) and sanctuary (Islington MHF, 1989). However, we know of no work that has asked the individual client at their time of most need what they want to happen to them. It might be argued that clients in crisis are not in a fit state to be asked what they want. This may in some circumstances be true; however, the claim of services that they are designed to meet users' needs cannot be substantiated unless they actually try to determine what they are. Services cannot claim to meet clients' needs without knowledge of what they are or whether they have been met/accounted for.

Coupled to this is the objective measurement of clients' service contacts. The suggestion of client tracking has to date been adopted by two services to our knowledge. In Bradford the mental health careers of clients referred to the home treatment service are being investigated through detailed, open-ended client interviews (Cohen, 1998). In Liverpool it is hoped it will be possible to compare clients' careers before and after their contact with the crisis service through access to Trust generated data (Liverpool City Council, 1996). We suggest here that this approach needs to be developed and that the mapping of clients' mental health careers is central to the evaluation of both crisis services in particular and mental health service provision as a whole.

It is suggested that the NHS patient number may be used to track mental health service users through the system of health service provision. All contacts with all services for all reasons may be catalogued on an electronic database so that client careers and possible patterns of illness can be elucidated. This process should indicate where, as we suspect, clients end up in crisis due to the inadequacies of the current systems in place.

Such a system might allow care induced crisis to be identified, for example, those caused by a lack of continuity of care, as might happen when a person is discharged on a Friday with no provision made for their care over the weekend; or when clients are not followed-up after their contact with a crisis service. If crises occur due to changes in medication where no provision was made in case of adverse consequences, this may be identified. Clients referred to crisis services can be monitored with respect to the reason for their referral, in order to see whether the services are targeting those that they aim to target or not. They can also be monitored in terms of the outcomes of their service contacts, such as whether they have avoided admission to hospital or not, in order to see if services are fulfilling their stated objectives.

Our work has suggested that follow-up and supports for clients after their crisis is essential if they are to avoid repeated problems (Hogan et al., 1997b). The tracking process could allow key workers to ascertain what is happening to their clients and whether or not they are receiving follow-up care. The aim of crisis intervention is that clients are helped to develop coping skills so that they are able to deal with future problems. It might be suggested that if a person is found to regularly suffer crises of a similar nature that they are not crises (when one is open to change) but rather psychiatric emergencies described by Jacobs as 'external situations requiring immediate action to prevent dire consequences' (1983, p. 27). Or, if clients are considered to be experiencing repeated crises, it might suggest the care received is either not implementing crisis intervention, or not doing it effectively.

There are ethical issues that surround the development and employment of these technologies, but at this distance there do seem to be clear benefits. For example, by identifying if and where services fail to integrate effectively so that services can be developed or targeted to fill these gaps. Tracking is not possible at the moment due to the lack of centralised record keeping across the mental health services. The process will also involve the initial outlay of significant resources in order to support: (a) the hardware necessary for computers to be compatible and networked; (b) the development of a suitable database to contain all the information generated in an easily recordable and accessible format; and (c) training to enable staff to be able to use the system. Nor would any results be immediately forthcoming. This is a long-term approach that could ultimately decrease the number of repeated crisis presentations in a client's mental health career through the identification of the causes of crises that can then be addressed.

Finally, the issue of client tracking is not the responsibility of crisis services alone. Crisis services cannot stand alone and achieve results for clients. They need services to refer clients on to, and services to refer to them. Mental health service provision needs to move on from operating as packets of different types of provision; in-patient versus home treatment, Social Services versus nursing care. Mental health service provision needs to adapt, integrate and become whole. Monetary, purchaser-provider and service boundaries need to be broken down so that users do not get lost in the system, nor the care they receive cause them more harm than good.

Conclusion

Research into psychiatric crisis services has been partial, local, not easily generalisable, of poor theoretical basis and usually not of experimental or quasi-experimental design. It is difficult to envisage either a randomised controlled trial or, indeed, homogenous services that would allow us to use the results of this same trial. Therefore service development and enhancement should be the focus; we need to see what works for whom and when.

Very briefly, the evaluation of mental health crisis services has been moving forwards. However, the views of service users need to be properly researched and accounted for. We suggest that client needs and wants at the beginning of each service contact, and what they want to be achieved through this service contact, can be measured. On discharge from a service, the client should be asked if they feel their needs have been met. Only in this way can services develop in such a way that they are able to meet clients' needs, and ultimately reduce the incidence of crises clients' experience. The future of evaluation research should be, we would argue, in developing methods that can be used by the majority of practitioners to enhance the services they deliver. For this purpose a richer definition of efficiency and a more inclusive model of effectiveness is required.

In sum, service evaluation needs to be incorporated into, and lead to, service development. Following the terminology used in education, the emphasis of such research needs to be focus on more formative than summative outcomes. Thereby producing evidence that is of use in improving services rather than indicating whether or not they give value for money. As part of that change in emphasis, it is important that the goals of a crisis service reflect the expectations of clients and that service users become more involved in the evaluation process.

Table 7.1   Summary of case studies

Place and type of service	Cost measurement method	Cost measurement outcome	Therapeutic effectiveness measurement method	Therapeutic effectiveness measurement outcome	Attempt to measure cost-effectiveness?
Huddersfield Crisis Intervention Team	Direct costs: traditional costs of six month in-patient stay; out-patient costs, crisis costs – travelling times, expenses, professional time with client.	Crisis intervention reported to be six times less expensive than traditional in-patient care.	Client functioning: GHQ-30 completed within one week of assessment and on discharge.	Improvement in symptoms between times one and two (no control group).	No.
	Indirect costs: relative's burden (SBAS), measured within one week of assessment and after two months.	Burden improved from time one to time two for C/T carers (no control group).	Hospital admissions: admissions in crisis consultant sector compared to three other sectors.	Decrease in admissions in crisis consultant's area. Steady increase in admissions in other areas.	
Maudsley Hospital (London) Daily Living Programme	Direct costs: service, accommodation costs.	Reported to be less in the DLP group than standard care group at four, 11 and 20 months.	Client functioning: GAS, PSE, SPRS, SAS, within 72 hours of entry, four, 11 and 20 months.	Both groups improved on all measures at four, 11 and 20 months. DLP group slightly superior at different times (GAS at four and 20 months, BPRS, PSE at 20 months).	Yes. DLP suggested to be more cost effective than standard in-patient care.
	Indirect costs: lost client employment.	No enumeration of same. No difference between DLP and control groups at baseline and 20 months.	Hospital admissions.	100% controls, 88% DLP group admitted, over 20 month period.	
	Family and informal costs (time, accommodation, etc.).	No enumeration of same. No difference in the amount of behaviours between the two groups.	Lengths of in-patient stay.	Reported to be 80% less in the DLP group.	

	Costs	Cost findings	Outcome measures	Outcome findings	
Sparkbrook Home Treatment Team	Direct costs: not considered. Indirect costs: carers' burden, SBAS, GHQ within ten days of patient admission, at one month and one year.	Similar scores for groups of SBAS at each time. No difference between groups on GHQ score at any time.	Client functioning: PSE (within three days of admission and at one year); Morningside Rehabilitation Scale (initial assessment and once a week for six weeks).	PSE scores in groups the same at baseline, and one year. No difference in Morningside scores apart from week two (Sparkbrook better).	No.
			Hospital admissions.	100% Small Heath clients admitted compared to 35% Sparkbrook clients.	
			Length of in-patient stay.	Shorter in Sparkbrook group.	
Wimbledon, Mitcham and Wandsworth – Dingleton model of community-based psychiatric care	Direct costs: in-patient, out-patient, service use, GP, social work, other obvious psychiatric contacts.	Home treatment group exhibited lower mean costs than the standard care group.	Client functioning: PSE, BPRS, SFS, clinical interview within two weeks of referral, six weeks, six and 12 months.	Clients in both groups improved in psychiatric and social functioning. No difference in the improvement of the groups at any assessment point.	No.
	Indirect costs: income, employment costs.	No enumeration of same reported. No difference between the groups.	Hospital admissions.	Fewer admissions and readmissions in the experimental group.	
	Family burden (informants reported problems with a list of activities).	Burden found to be low in carers and similar in carers of both groups of clients.	Length of in-patient stay.	Experimental group clients had shorter lengths of stay than the controls.	

References

Beech, P. and Norman, I.J. (1995), 'Patients' perceptions of the quality of psychiatric nursing care: findings from a small-scale descriptive study', *Journal of Clinical Nursing*, Vol. 4, pp. 117–23.
Beeforth, M., Conlan, F., Field, V., Hoser, B. and Sayce, L. (1990), *Whose service is it anyway? Users' views on co-ordinating community care*, Research and Development for Psychiatry, London.
Beer, D., Cope, S., Smith, J. and Smith, R. (1995), 'The crisis team as part of comprehensive local services', *Psychiatric Bulletin*, Vol. 19, pp. 616–19.
Burns, T. (1997), Personal communication.
Burns, T., Beadsmoore, A., Bhat, A.V., Oliver, A. and Mathers, C. (1993), 'A controlled trial of home-based acute psychiatric services I: clinical and social outcome', *British Journal of Psychiatry*, Vol. 163, pp. 49–54.
Burns, T., Raftery, J., Beadsmoore, A., McGuigan, S. and Dickson, M. (1993), 'A controlled trial of home-based acute psychiatric services II: treatment patterns and costs', *British Journal of Psychiatry*, Vol. 163, pp. 55–61.
Caplan, G. (1964), *Principles of Preventive Psychiatry*, Basic Books, New York.
Cobb, A. (1995), 'Crisis? What crisis?', *Health Service Journal*, 12 January, pp. 22–3.
Cohen, B.M.Z. (1998), Personal communication.
Croft-Jeffreys, C. and Wilkinson, G. (1989), 'Estimated costs of neurotic disorder in UK general practice', *Psychological Medicine*, Vol. 19, pp. 549–58, cited by Burns et al. (1993b), op. cit.
Davis, A., Newton, S. and Smith, D. (1985), 'Coventry Crisis Intervention Team: The Consumer's View', *Social Services Research*, Vol. 14, pp. 7–32.
Dean, C. and Gadd, E.M. (1990), 'Home treatment for acute psychiatric illness', *British Medical Journal*, Vol. 301, pp. 1021–3.
Dean, C., Phillips, J., Gadd, M., Joseph, M. and England, S. (1993), 'Comparison of community based service with hospital based service for people with acute, severe psychiatric illness', *British Medical Journal*, Vol. 307, pp. 473–6.
Department of Health (1994), *Mental Illness* (2nd edition), HMSO, London.
Hobbs, M. (1984), 'Crisis intervention in theory and practice: a selective review', *British Journal of Medical Psychology*, Vol. 57, pp. 23–34.
Hogan, K., Crawford-Wright, A., Orme, S., Easthope, Y. and Barker, D. (1997a), *Walsall Crisis Support Service. Final Report. Volume 1 Literature Review*, Psychology Division, University of Wolverhampton.
Hogan, K., Crawford-Wright, A., Orme, S., Easthope, Y. and Barker, D. (1997b), *Walsall Crisis Support Service. Final Report. Volume 2. Service Evaluation*, Psychology Division, University of Wolverhampton.
Hogan, K. and Orme, S. (1997), 'The effectiveness of crisis services: a review of research', in *Proceedings of the 2nd Annual Conference on Crisis Services*, University of Leeds.
Holloway, F. (1993), 'The user perspective on mental health services: its value and limitations', in Leiper, R. and Field, V. (eds), *Counting for Something in Mental Health Service: Effective User Feedback*, Avebury, Aldershot.
Hoult, J. (1986), 'Community care of the acutely mentally ill', *British Journal of Psychiatry*, Vol. 149, pp. 137–44.
Islington Mental Health Forum (1989), *Fit For Consumption? Mental Health Users' Views of Treatment in Islington*, Islington Mental Health Forum, London.
Jacobs, D. (1983), 'The treatment capabilities of psychiatric emergency services', *General Open Psychiatry*, Vol. 5, pp. 171–7.
Jones, D. (1987), 'Community Psychiatry in the Borders', in Drucker, N. (ed.), *Creating Community Mental Health Services in Scotland Volume 2: Community Services in Practice*, Scottish Association for Mental Health.

Knapp, M., Beecham, J., Koutsogeorgopoulou, V., Hallam, A., Fenyo, A., Marks, I.M., Connolly, J., Audini, B. and Muijen, M. (1994), 'Service use and costs of home-based versus hospital-based care for people with serious mental illness', *British Journal of Psychiatry*, Vol. 165, pp. 195–203.

Kwakwa, J. (1995), 'Alternatives to hospital-based mental health care', *Nursing Times*, Vol. 91, pp. 38–9.

Liverpool City Council (1996), *Liverpool Mental Health Crisis Service, Progress Report, August 1996*, City of Liverpool Social Services Department, Liverpool.

Mant, D. (1997), *R&D in Primary Care: National Working Group Report*, NHS Executive, South and West.

Marks, I.M., Connolly, J., Muijen, M., Audini, B., McNamee, G. and Lawrence, R.E. (1994), 'Home-based versus hospital-based care for people with serious mental illness', *British Journal of Psychiatry*, Vol. 165, pp. 179–94.

McCrone, P. and Weich, S. (1996), 'Mental health care costs: paucity of measurement', in Thornicroft, C. and Tansella, M. (eds), *Mental Health Outcome Measures*, Springer-Verlag, Berlin.

Muijen, M., Marks, I.M., Connolly, J., Audini, B. and McNamee, G. (1992), 'The Daily Living Programme: preliminary comparison of community versus hospital-based treatment for the seriously mentally ill facing emergency admission', *British Journal of Psychiatry*, Vol. 160, pp. 370–84.

Orme, S. and Hogan, K. (forthcoming), *A nationwide survey of the provision of crisis services*.

Parkes, C.M. (1992a), 'Services for families in crisis in Tower Hamlets: evaluations by general practitioners and social workers', *Psychiatric Bulletin*, Vol. 16, pp. 748–50.

Parkes, C.M. (1992b), 'Perceptions of a crisis service by referrers and clients', *Psychiatric Bulletin*, Vol. 16, pp. 751–3.

Punukollu, N.R. (1991), 'Huddersfield (West) crisis intervention team: four years follow-up', *Psychiatric Bulletin*, Vol. 15, pp. 278–80.

Ratna, L. (1996), 'The theoretical basis of crisis therapy', in Tomlinson, D. (ed.), *Alternatives to Hospital for People in Crisis. Papers from a Conference held at Leeds University 18-9-96*, School of Health and Social Care, South Bank University, London.

Renshaw, J. (1989), 'Crisis Intervention: Introduction', in Renshaw, J. (ed.), *Crisis Intervention Services Information Pack*, Good Practices in Mental Health, London.

Ricketts, T. (1992), 'Consumer satisfaction surveys in mental health', *British Journal of Nursing*, Vol. 1, pp. 523–7.

Ruggeri, M. (1996), 'Satisfaction with psychiatric services', in Thornicroft, G. and Tansella, M. (eds), *Mental Health Outcome Measures*, Springer-Verlag, Berlin.

Sharma, T., Carson, J. and Berry, C. (1992), 'Patient voices', *Health Service Journal*, 16 January, pp. 20–21.

Spencer, A. (1996), 'Using consumer feedback to improve services', *International Journal of Health Care Quality Assurance*, Vol. 9, pp. 29–33.

Uchtenhagen, A. (1986), 'Evaluation of Community Services', *Acta Psychiatrica Belg.*, Vol. 86, pp. 350–61.

Value for Money Unit, NHS Wales (1997), 'Mental Health Crisis Services Information Directory for Service Providers', Welsh Health Common Services Authority, Cardiff.

Waldron, C. (1989), 'Crisis Intervention: A Persistent Theme', in Renshaw, J. (ed.), *Crisis Intervention Service Information Pack*, Good Practices in Mental Health, London.

Williams, B. (1995), 'Users' views of community mental health care', in Crosby, C. and Barry, M.M. (eds), *Community Care: Evaluation of the Provision of Mental Health Services*, Avebury, Aldershot.

Yuen, F. (1994), 'Evaluations in mental health services: some methodological considerations', *Journal of Nursing Management*, Vol. 2, pp. 287–91.

8 Community Psychiatric Nursing's Role in Managing Crises

PAUL GODIN AND CHRISTOPHER SCANLON

Introduction

Histories of the management of madness typically devote little attention to the role of mental nursing, usually concentrating upon the development of policy and the practices of mental medicine; though Carpenter's (1985) history of the Confederation of Health Service Employees (COHSE) (once the main trade union of mental nurses) and Nolan's (1993) history of mental nursing are notable exceptions. This chapter is thus, in part, an attempt to make mental nursing more visible by highlighting its roles in the development of crisis services in the post-Second World War period. Firstly, we offer an account of how mental nursing transformed its care practices within a changing British asylum system, shifting the focus of work into the community. Secondly, we consider how community psychiatric nursing became a distinct sub-specialism of mental nursing and how community psychiatric nurses (CPNs) developed their role and function. Particular consideration will be given to the major influence that Caplan's (1964) model of preventive psychiatry and crisis theory have had upon the development of CPNs' practice.

The Transformation of Mental Nursing

The long term move towards greater incorporation of the asylum system into mainstream health was boosted considerably by the nationalisation of health services in 1948. Asylums, already renamed as mental hospitals under the 1930 Mental Treatment Act, were able to make an even stronger claim to be similar to general hospitals in their operation and purpose. Mental medicine attempted to promote such an image through its greater use of physical

102

treatments, such as insulin therapy, electroconvulsive therapy (ECT) and psychosurgery. More significantly mental medicine initiated reforms in the treatment regimes, administration and social organisation of the asylums; such practices as have become known as 'social psychiatry'. Doors were unlocked; patients were engaged in occupation geared towards their rehabilitation (gardening, knitting, letter writing, etc.), rather than the maintenance of the institution (laundering, cleaning, mucking out); and freedoms were encouraged for nursing staff and patients in democratic 'therapeutic community' regimes which were designed to achieve more effective treatment. In this demo-cratisation process the mental patient's social persona had been rediscovered along with the nurse to patient relationship, which was thenceforward seen as the major means towards the resurrection of the person within the patient. Thus the nurse to patient relationship took on a major clinical significance within the new regime of social therapy. No longer were the patient and mental nurse merely parts of the harsh disciplinary machinery of the asylum (described so depressingly by Lomax (1921) in his expose of Prestwich Asylum). The mental nurse was from this point on, in a limited fashion, to be engaged in psychotherapeutic activities with the patient, the main objective being to rehabilitate the mental patient back into work and the community. As Armstrong (1983) points out, this invention of the nurse to patient relationship only occurred much later in general nursing, with the development of nursing models and the nursing process. Though the old regime of authoritarian, hierarchical, regulatory discipline was far from dead, the new order was sufficiently influential to bring about considerable change. The throughput of patients (i.e., the total number of admissions to, and discharges from hospital during any given period) increased, aided by the development of psychiatric out-patient clinics, domiciliary visiting and the development of day hospitals. It was in association with these practices that community psychiatric nursing (then referred to as 'out-patient nursing') first began.

The First Community Psychiatric Nurses

Notably, out-patient mental nursing arose from within hospitals that were pioneering social psychiatry, where the nurse to patient relationship was recognised to have therapeutic value. The handful of mental nurses that worked in the community in the 1950s assisted in out-patient clinics, followed up patients that failed to attend such clinics and visited patients at home in place of out-patient appointments. They also assisted in the running of social activities for discharged patients in the day hospitals. Other functions they were reported to have had were in giving advice and support to out-patients and their carers, as well as supervising patients' medication and hygiene. However it was made quite clear, in articles that reported about 'out-patient nursing' (Moore, 1964; May, 1965), that these mental nurses working in the community were merely practising the same skills as those which they practised in the hospital, since they gave continuing care to chronically disabled discharged patients. The difference between the role of the CPN and the social worker though, was clearly delineated. Moore (1965) suggested that the nurse's approach was primarily clinical and did not involve detailed consideration of the patient's family or attempt to change the patient's social environment.

At a social work conference in 1969 Smith, a spokesperson for the Psychiatric Social Workers' Association, gave the following guarded approval of the new role of the mental nurse in the community:

> There is at present a role for the nurse outside the hospital within the limits of his present training. This is confined to educational and practical and therapeutic functions towards patients with organic or chronic disorder with whom he had already built up a relationship in hospital, and to patients in group situations. If some additional training were given, for instance in inter-personal relationships and in the use of the social services, he would be able to expand his work towards those who are less chronically disabled (cited in Sladden, 1979, p. 49).

Clearly these early CPNs were seen as useful in managing the after care of chronically disabled out-patients; a client group whose needs were thought to only require basic caring skills. This practice of mental nurses working in the community increased during the 1960s, such that a survey in 1966 found there to be 42 hospitals employing some 225 mental nurses working in such settings; though only 26 of them worked exclusively in the community (Royal College of Nursing, 1966).

The 1960s also witnessed a clear policy in Britain towards the decline of the asylum system and the creation of community care. In the United States of America (USA) community care policy was far more radical. In the USA the 1963 Community Mental Health Centre Act effectively gave psychiatry a mandate to treat the entire population. To enable traditional psychiatry to meet this challenge Caplan (1964) offered his blueprint of 'preventive psychiatry', which centrally incorporated Lindeman's (1944) theory of crisis intervention. However, in Britain, as Rogers and Pilgrim (1996) argue, the policy of community mental health care, articulated in the Hospital Plan for England and Wales (Ministry of Health, 1962), proved to be more rhetoric than reality.

Though the psychiatric in-patient population continued to decline, psychiatric admissions increased. The British community mental health care policy was more to do with re-institutionalisation, from the old asylums to psychiatric units within the new district general hospitals, than about establishing an infrastructure for community care as an alternative to hospital. A Ministry of Health Report entitled *Psychiatric Nursing Today and Tomorrow* (1968) firmly located the nub of modern mental nursing to be within the psychiatric units of district general hospitals, saying nothing about the development of community psychiatric nursing.

Community Psychiatric Nurses in the 1970s and the Influences of Caplan

Caplan's model of preventive psychiatry and crisis theory only slowly filtered into some of the rather patchy practices of community mental health care in Britain. The ideas of Caplan and crisis theory only influenced CPNs' development as they began to mature into a distinct sub-specialism of mental nursing. The 1970s was a decade in which community psychiatric nursing noticeably came of age as a professionalising occupation, with its development as an activity performed by mental nurses specialising in this work (increasingly referred to as CPNs) rather than as an occasional activity of ward nurses. Furthermore, CPNs developed their own staff association (the Community Psychiatric Nurses' Association (CPNA)), and their own post registration training, together with new methods of practice in new settings. The 1970s also saw the introduction of the Local Authority Social Services Act (DHSS, 1970), through which the recommendations of the report of the Inter-Departmental Committee on the organisation of social services in England and Wales (1968) (better known as the Seebohm report) were implemented. This Act made provision for psychiatric social workers to be redeployed from mental hospitals to social services area teams and made social work generic in its practice. Although often continuing to be based in mental hospitals, social workers were no longer under the organisational control of hospital boards. Social work was effectively establishing its own independent power base and professional, independent identity, in the practice of psychosocial 'case work'. Bereft of the erstwhile ready support of this paramedical profession, psychiatrists increasingly looked towards community psychiatric nurses as an alternative occupational group to patronise. As a Royal Medico-Psychological Association report in 1969 put it:

It is likely that a new body of mental health social workers would have to be evolved to fill the gap left by the destruction of the present growing services, perhaps with an enhanced medical or nursing background (cited in Simmons and Brooker, 1986, pp. 43–4).

The growth of CPNs was rapid during this decade. Parnell (1974) conducted the first major survey of community psychiatric nursing in Britain to find that 714 mental nurses were working in the community within 417 schemes. By 1980 the first CPN census found there to be 1,667 full time CPNs in Britain (White, 1993). Parnell's study had found CPNs to be variously employed and located, working exclusively or occasionally within the community. As the decade progressed debate ensued as to the relative merits of either releasing hospital nurses to work into the community on an occasional basis or to employ nurses to work exclusively in the community. Advocates of the former argued that it made for greater continuity of care and that ward staff benefited from community experience. However, Sharpe (1975) argued that patients' dependence upon the hospital was fostered by such arrangements. Leopoldt (1974) clearly pointed out how impractical occasional community nursing became the more it was practised. The logistics of maintaining a caseload in the community whilst being committed simultaneously to ward work were impossible to resolve. Thus CPN practice developed increasingly as a full time specialist activity.

The introduction of phenothiazines in the 1950s had first been seen as merely a useful way of controlling behaviour within the hospital. During the 1960s their long term use was increasingly regarded to be effective in reducing the relapse of discharged patients that had been diagnosed as schizophrenic. However compliance was problematic. In the late 1960s the development of long acting phenothiazine injections (Moditen and Modecate) meant that patients no longer had to be relied upon to orally consume these drugs. To begin with, psychiatrists administered these depot injections in out-patient clinics. However, they were quick to delegate the task to nurses and it soon became a primary task of many CPNs. Primacy was given to these drugs in several respects. They were increasingly proclaimed as the main factor in bringing about a declining psychiatric in-patient population. They also became seen as fundamental in the treatment of discharged patients and the basis for many CPN services established at this time. Many CPNs spent their time almost exclusively administering injections to many patients that they only momentarily encountered. One CPN recollects what his CPN practice was like in the 1970s thus:

... all we did was inject people. There were three of us and we had roughly 600 people who were on injections, and we had depot clinics nearly every day of the week, plus home visits. On Wednesday we had a clinic from 9 a.m. until 7.30 p.m. ... The people were queuing up, there was no system to it. (Godin and Scanlon, 1997, p. 79)

The rather dehumanising, reductively biomedical nature of such practice earned CPNs disparaging nicknames such as: 'the modecate man (woman)' and 'the flying needle'. Where community psychiatric nursing was practised as an occasional activity of ward staff, the introduction of injections increased such practice. Ward staff were frequently away from the hospital to administer injections to discharged patients. Warren (1971), a nursing officer at Herrison Hospital (Dorchester), attempted to address the criticism that such practice was wasteful by reference to value gained in averting the relapse and admission of patients in receipt of these injections. However it was rather an example of the impracticality of continuing to use ward nurses for community nursing.

Despite this new function of injection giving, that community psychiatric nursing had acquired, CPNs were at the same time beginning to transcend the 'after-care' and 'clinical' tasks role they had begun with. They began to specialise in a variety of aspects of their practice and, with specific client groups such as children and the elderly, to take part in experimental initiatives. The theory of crisis intervention and preventative psychiatry played a major part in this development. A number of crisis intervention services developed in the 1970s in which CPNs were involved. As the quasi professional group emerging to fill the gap left by psychiatric social workers, CPNs used crisis intervention theory and preventive psychiatry to inform their own development in primary care.

CPNs in Crisis Intervention Teams

From within hospitals that operated regimes informed by social psychiatry, a number of crisis intervention services arose. The best example of such services is perhaps that of Dingleton Hospital. This had been one of the first hospitals to operate a comprehensive open door policy in the 1940s. In the 1960s the sexual segregation of its wards was abolished as they were transformed into therapeutic communities. In 1969 CPNs were employed within newly established multidisciplinary crisis teams. Nursing accounts of the service (Stobie and Hopkins, 1972; McDonald, 1972) emphasise how the development of a crisis service in the community was seen as a transplantation of the same ideas and practices that prevailed within the parent hospital. The idea that the patient's suffering can largely be understood as the result of psychosocial factors, and ameliorated through the management of the environment and social relations surrounding him/her, was seen as common to both therapeutic community regimes and crisis intervention work. It was only the centre of treatment, which had become the home rather than the hospital, that had changed. However, the dangers of a potential transfer of the treatment regime of the parent hospital to staff practices in patients' homes were also clearly understood within nursing at the time. As McDonald (1972, p. 83), who was then nursing officer responsible for CPNs at Dingleton, presciently put it:

> ... the role of any hospital discipline in the community will be an extension of its hospital role ... if nurses treat patients as dependent children with varying degrees of pathological symptoms to be ameliorated only by medication, their community role will be similar as perhaps the current trend to use nurses as Modecate injectors would seem to indicate. Are we making the best use of well-trained nurses in psychiatry? Are nurses receiving appropriate training for the changing role of psychiatry?

The democratisation of therapy that characterised both therapeutic communities and crisis intervention services led to questions about the appropriate role of mental nurses and their training. Nurses were acting as members of teams in which roles were blurred; making shared social rather than medical diagnosis; and participating in therapeutic endeavours based on a knowledge of family and marital therapy, group dynamics, and other specialist interventions. Their taking up of these roles raised the questions of: (a) whether such nurses were doing anything that could specifically be called nursing; and (b) whether they were adequately trained for what they were doing.

From case examples of nurses involvement in crisis work at Dingleton (Stobie and Hopkins, 1972; McDonald, 1972), it would seem that these CPNs were integrally involved in this crisis intervention service. However at Napsbury Hospital crisis intervention lacked nurse involvement. In a *Nursing Times* article Farewell (1974), then the Consultant Psychiatrist of the crisis service, bemoaned the absence of nurses, arguing that though all disciplines have a major shared function within the team, each has a unique contribution to make, nursing's being that of 'intimate contact'.

Pullen and Gilbert (1979) report on an interesting experiment in the running of wards in the Royal Edinburgh Hospital. Though all the wards operated therapeutic community regimes, the democratisation of therapy was limited such that all out-patient work, and all individual psychotherapy was carried out exclusively by doctors. Admissions and discharges were solely decided by doctors. The experiment was based on the greater involvement of ward nurses in follow up visits to discharged patients, and on their undertaking of individual psychotherapy. They were also more involved in decisions about hospital admissions and discharges. This was brought about through their taking responsibility for the management and organisation of individual care by means of a system for the allocation of patients to a 'named nurse'. One of the results of the experiment was that the lengths of admissions were noticeably reduced. As the scheme was extended to other wards, the theory and practice of crisis intervention were employed to support it. The scheme particularly changed the process of admissions. General practitioner (GP) referrals for out-patient appointments were responded to by home visits, undertaken by a multi-disciplinary crisis team of the ward, which naturally included ward nurses. Overall, it was an attempt to make the hospital become more community focused and out-reaching in its practices.

As with any new initiative, the protagonists of crisis intervention schemes felt compelled to justify their practices through reference to its cost benefits. In reports about their services, cited above, there is abundant reference as to how early intervention enabled people to satisfactorily resolve crisis and avert unnecessary miserable careers as mental patients, ostracised from their families and society. Case examples provide very convincing evidence to suggest that such work had considerable value. Reference was also made to supporting quantitative data. Stobie and Hopkins (1972) point out that whilst admissions to mental hospitals increased by 150 per cent in England and Wales from 1959 to 1969 the admission rate to Dingleton Hospital had decreased in 1971 by 8 per cent from what it had been in 1959. Furthermore they questioned the efficacy of the alternative; namely the enormous growth of psychiatric out-patient clinics, that they suggest, attend to patients in a brief and superficial fashion.

CPNs in Primary Care

Whilst some CPNs were becoming integral members of crisis teams others were beginning to operate independently of mental hospitals or specialist services that operated from them, as fairly autonomous practitioners within primary health care. In Oxford, from 1972 onwards, a number of CPNs were seconded to work half their time within health centres and GP practices. The change of location made for a change in role for the CPN as GPs and other primary health care workers referred clients to them. Leopoldt (1979), the nursing officer in charge of the project, found that GPs not only referred patients to CPNs that they would have otherwise referred to consultant psychiatrists or out-patients but also referred a significant number of patients that would have otherwise been left or seen only occasionally by GPs. Leopoldt thus argued that CPNs had made advances in the practice of preventive psychiatry through their primary health care attachments in several ways. For in seeing patients that otherwise would have not received any mental health care, CPNs were engaged in crisis prevention, averting the need for crisis intervention. Furthermore close working relationships between CPNs and primary health care workers enabled the latter to become more confident in their own dealings with mental health problems. Alternatives were sometimes found to that of referring patients to consultant psychiatrists and to an ensuing admission to mental hospital.

CPNs' greater involvement in primary health care, both through attachments and their taking referrals directly from GPs and other primary health care workers, increased throughout the 1980s. In 1985, 28.3 per cent of CPNs' client referrals came from GPs and district nurses; by 1990 this had increased to 39.7 per cent (White, 1993). In primary health care CPNs acted with a relatively high degree of clinical autonomy as they assessed and cared for clients referred to them, independently of psychiatrists.

As with CPNs working in crisis teams, CPNs working in primary health care were ill equipped to do such work through their traditional nurse training. Post-registration CPN training began in the 1970s and by the end of the decade had taken the form of a one year course. In what might be regarded as the first text book for CPNs, Carr et al. (1980) outlined principles of 'preventive psychiatric nursing', based upon Caplan's work, as a model for CPNs' development, that they argued must be: '… in the direction of true "primary" care …'. They presented Caplan's model as a theoretical rationale for practical interventions which could be linked to the use of the 'nursing process' (a system of patient care that was then just finding its feet within British nursing). This text also emphasised the difference of approach inherent within the form of preventive mental health promotion being advocated. Its focus was on a psychosocial understanding of mental illness, rather than upon the illness and cure approach of traditional psychiatry, which was more biomedically orientated. Clearly CPNs' practice was in both camps: for they continued to act as injection givers whilst at the same time were ever more engaged in crisis and early prevention work within primary health care. Yet Caplan's model of prevention could be drawn on to reconcile these divergent practices. For it was consistent with both the established CPN role in after-care and injection administration, which might well be construed as a form of tertiary prevention, and the novel CPN role in taking general practice referrals, which could be considered to be a form of secondary prevention.

CPNs in the 1980s

By the 1980s Caplan's model had stimulated CPNs' imagination as to how they could develop their practice in new areas of illness prevention and mental health promotion. Some saw the latter as the very essence of community psychiatric nursing. Hendon (1983), proclaimed that: 'community psychiatric nursing is the only professional discipline whose primary concern is the promotion of mental health in the community'. Informed by the concept of primary health care promotion, Higgins (1984) describes how he and his CPN colleagues became involved in teaching mental health issues in a local secondary school. However such CPN involvement in this kind of primary prevention seems rare.

In what could be regarded as the second CPN text book Simmons and Brooker (1986) outline crisis intervention as a principle that could largely inform the practice of CPNs engaged in short term work within primary health care. Yet despite the rapidly increasing number of CPNs and their growing confidence to develop their practice, reservations were expressed about what they were doing. Not very surprisingly, Consultant Psychiatrists felt they were losing control of CPNs in primary care and recommended that CPNs should always maintain their base in the hospital mental health team (Royal College of Psychiatrists, 1980). From within community psychiatric nursing, doubts were expressed as to whether CPNs were able to take on this new role of preventive mental health care. In a study of CPN practice Skidmore (1986) concludes that CPNs lacked skills in effective counselling, family work, etc. and were thus not able to adequately practice secondary prevention. This, he argues, was not simply because too few CPNs had undertaken CPN training, since those who had trained proved to be no more competent in such skills than those who had not. Other academic specialists in nursing similarly emphasised inadequacies in CPNs' professional knowledge and therapeutic competence (Sladden, 1979; Pollock, 1989). Nevertheless, research into CPN practice during the 1980s indicated that there was some evidence to suggest that CPNs could be effective in secondary prevention. In primary health care Robertson and Scott (1985) found CPNs to be effective in the care of patients diagnosed as suffering from mood disturbance; Brooking and Minghella (1987) found CPNs to be more effective than psychiatrists in the care of parasuicidal patients; and Storer et al. (1987) found CPNs to be effective in the care of people with mental health problems that presented themselves in Accident and Emergency Departments. The extent to which GPs came to value and to utilise CPNs in the 1980s, with respect to the care of people with emotional problems, is further indication of CPNs' involvement (and perhaps even therapeutic competence) in early intervention and crisis work within primary health care. Surveys of GPs' experience of CPNs (White, 1986; Godin and Wilson, 1986) generally indicate that GPs commonly referred patients to CPNs for this purpose. Typically GPs reported CPNs and the immediate psycho-therapeutic care they offered to be a better alternative to prescribing minor tranquillisers or referral to psychiatrists for many patients that they saw.

The 1990 CPN census (White, 1993) showed that by the end of the 1980s CPNs were undertaking a substantial amount of early intervention work, through their ever strengthening links with GPs. The census also reveals a number of other ways in which CPNs could be seen to be engaged in crisis management. Firstly, about half of CPN services offered out-of-hours care (evenings and weekends) that were mostly organised to deal with emergency or crisis calls only (Lee, 1990). The rationale for such provision can be argued to have been, to a certain extent, informed by crisis theory, with CPNs recognising the importance of a rapid response to emotional crisis in order to support clients coping abilities.

Secondly, the 1990 census showed that CPNs had grown in number to nearly 5,000 distributed fairly evenly throughout Britain (White, 1993). CPNs had by now established a certain presence within most communities and primary health care services. CPNs were thus well placed to undertake crisis intervention when disaster struck Lockerbie in 1988. Carlisle (1990) describes how the three CPNs whose area patch happened to be within Lockerbie quickly found themselves involved in seeing those who had been bereaved by the tragedy and those who had been traumatised by rescue work. The CPNs describe how they attempted to normalise rather than pathologise people's experiences, and the way in which they operated through an informal referral system. They also discuss their participation in the running of a 24-hour phone assistance line.

Thirdly, the census revealed an increasing number of CPNs reporting specialism in particular therapeutic approaches (family therapy, counselling, cognitive therapy, etc.); a degree of specialism which can be taken as an indicator of their increasing therapeutic competence to undertake crisis work. The census also attempted to measure the areas in which CPNs specialised. Though the census does not record the number of CPNs working within Accident and Emergency departments, from the growing literature reporting on such work (Storer et al., 1987; Atha, 1990), it would seem that this was increasing becoming a specialist area of CPN practice. Given the distress of many of those attending Accident and Emergency Departments, (people suffering physical ill health and trauma; people that have attempted suicide or otherwise harmed themselves; people that may be described as being 'psychiatric emergencies'; etc.) it is easy to see the benefits and appropriateness of a crisis orientated approach in this setting. The findings of Storer et al. (1987) indicate that CPNs acting in such a role within an accident and emergency department were effective in treating attendees. CPN care reduced demand for other services, indicating a more positive and adaptive resolution of the patient's crisis. (Mental nurses involvement in crisis work within Accident and Emergency departments is discussed in greater detail in the next chapter.)

Lastly, the 1990 CPN census also revealed there to be 101 CPNs specialising in the care of children and adolescents. Services in this area have traditionally taken a very family and psycho-educational approach. It is thus hardly surprising that in a small scale study by Bune (1985) it was found that CPNs specialising in this area, more than other areas of CPN practice, considered that a large part of their work was associated with reducing the incidence of new cases of mental illness.

Though policy and practice towards community mental health care was much slower in Britain than in the USA, two developments in Britain in the direction of community care particularly characterised the latter part of the 1980s. Firstly, the asylums eventually began to shut down under a firm closure programme. This in turn gave rise to an increase in rehabilitation and resettlement, which became a growing specialism amongst CPNs (some 231 CPNs being engaged as specialists in such work by the time of the 1990 CPN census (White, 1993)).

Secondly, a rather ad hoc mushrooming of community mental health centres (CMHCs) occurred (from an estimated 20 CMHCs in 1985 to 81 in 1990 (Sayce et al., 1991)). CMHCs had been the building block of the USA's policy for comprehensive community mental health care, that was at best a limited success. Similarly the British emulation of the USA system too had its failings. Though British CMHCs commonly claimed, with reference to Caplan's model of preventive psychiatry, to provide comprehensive mental health care for everybody, they were clearly limited in their operation. As they attended to the needs of people in crisis they were accused of doing so at the expense of the needs of people with long term mental health (Sayce et al., 1991). Furthermore interdisciplinary tension about objectives and teamwork failure were noted (Goldie et al., 1989; Sayce et al. 1991). The literature suggests that CPNs were not always integral members of CMHCs. Patmore and Weaver (1991) found that when CPNs joined CMHC teams, CMHC managers were often reluctant to incorporate CPNs' caseloads of long term clients into that of the CMHC. Also Morrall (1995) found that CPNs were reluctant to bring referrals from GPs of people suffering emotional problems to the CMHC team, preferring to covertly manage such cases themselves. This suggests that CPNs were unwilling to give up the functional autonomy and respect they had achieved within primary health care in exchange for the benefits of full membership of the CMHC team.

CPNs in the 1990s

The 1990s has seen a major change in community mental health policy that has made for major changes in the practices of most mental health professionals. Accordingly preventive psychiatry and crisis theory have had to take on a meaning to fit their new world. In this part of the chapter we briefly consider how mental health care has become so different in the 1990s from that which preceded it and assess how this change has affected the practice of CPNs.

Firstly, the dissaggregation of the planning and providing parts of the NHS, together with the development of welfare pluralism, have made for a market discipline that has fundamentally changed the way CPNs work. Once expanding into primary care, taking referrals from anybody, CPNs now provide services only to those who have contracted for it. Thus GPs, who once referred emotionally disturbed patients to CPNs at no cost, now find that such service is at a price. They have thus turned to practice counsellors and practice nurses to perform this function.

Secondly, CPNs are now largely reserved for what is being proclaimed as the more important function of caring for the 'severely mentally ill'. A string of health policy legislation, from the Community Care White Paper (Department of Health – DoH, 1989) onwards, has directed all mental health professionals towards prioritising this client group. This direction was also supported by evidence from a study by Gournay and Brooking (1994), which suggested that less severely mentally ill patients receiving CPN care had no better outcomes than those receiving normal GP care. This study has been much quoted to suggest that CPNs were a wasted resource in this area, as any preventive work that they felt they might be doing was in fact illusionary in terms of its efficacy. Furthermore, the DoH (1994a) damned CPNs for their neglect of the severely mentally ill, pointing out that the 1990 CPN census (White, 1993) had revealed that only 20 per cent of people diagnosed as schizophrenic in England were being seen by CPNs, whilst as many as one in four CPNs claimed to be without any schizophrenic clients on their caseloads. The report also stated that:

> ... the essential focus for the work of the mental health nurse lies in working with people with serious or enduring mental illness in secondary and tertiary care... (p. 49).

CPNs were being encouraged to abandon their position in primary care and their less severely mentally ill clients to assume a new role in the systems of case management that had been introduced through the NHS and Community Care Act (DoH, 1990). Case management arose in the USA in the 1970s and might be described as a method of managing all services and other aspects of disabled peoples' lives in an efficient and effective manner such that they are able to survive in the community. Psychiatric rehabilitation, under social psychiatry, had been a matter of processing mental patients from the hospital to the community and giving basic after-care. The community management of 'chronic' mental patients was now seen as needing far more organisation and coordination than had been previously realised. If done well it could avert the need for hospital admission. The new practices of 'case management' were thus more about enabling mental patients to successfully live in the community without having to be admitted to hospital.

In the UK, case management was split into 'care management', under which social services managed social care, and the 'care programme approach' (CPA), which was an over arching system, led by health services, for managing the lives of mental patients in the community. The responsibilities given to health care workers (such as psychiatrists, who now found themselves to be 'responsible medical officers' to discharged patients) under these systems of case management, have given rise to the nationwide development of community mental health teams (Onyett et al., 1994, found 517 in England). Under CPA, packages of care for mental patients in the community are administered by a key worker, who is central to its implementation and success. As the majority occupational group in community mental health work, CPNs find themselves most frequently assuming this role. These systems perhaps stress the need to 'manage' rather than 'enable' those they attend to. As concerns about the dangerous potential of mental patients in the community have grown, more insistent and coercive measures of management have been introduced in the care of mental patients. 'Assertive outreach', an aggressive form of intensive case management (commonly described as being built on the principle of never taking 'no' for answer from clients), is seen by some as a model of good practice; perhaps, as McFayden and Vincent (1998) suggest, to be applied to all mental patients that are particularly at risk of suicide, committing acts of violence towards others, and serious self neglect. Formal methods of supervision, such as the supervision register (DoH, 1994b) and supervised discharge (DoH, 1995) have been introduced to monitor and restrict the behaviour of patients in the community, giving new statutory powers to CPNs over their clients. At the time of writing (August 1998) the Minister for Health has stated that community care has 'failed' and that there is a need for a 'third way', between failed community care and a return to the asylum. Such views indicate that the review of community mental health care which has been initiated by the Minister is likely to give even greater weight to a policy of supervision, control and management of the danger that mental patients in the community putatively pose to others. In short what might be regarded as an asylumization within the community is occurring. In such a regime Morrall (1998) suggests CPNs might exploit their position to claim a vital key role in the policing of the mad in the community.

Conclusion

In this chapter we have illustrated the way in which nurses took a prominent role in the democratisation of therapy within the old asylums, and how they developed out-patient nursing in order to extend that process into the community. We have seen that nurse innovators of the period were sensitive to the dangers of over-supervision and of taking away responsibilities from patients in the community, after the same fashion as had been the traditional practice in hospital. This they clearly identified as both authoritarian and anti-therapeutic.

We have also examined the development of community psychiatric nursing as an occupational specialism which grasped the opportunities for early intervention and primary preventive work with mental patients where these became available through attachments to GPs and direct referrals from that quarter. Evidence has been presented to indicate that in many instances CPNs moved on from being flying needles to become skilled practitioners in the management of personal mental health crises in the community. GPs appeared to be particularly satisfied with the response which they could obtain from CPNs for the patients on their lists.

However, we also noted that questions have been raised in recent years about the legitimacy of CPNs undertaking a variety of specialist counselling and therapeutic roles, given that the training they received to support such work could not be demonstrated to have made them more effective in it. We also noted the tendency of psychiatrists to lobby for CPNs to be brought back within their sphere of influence rather than that of the GP.

The context for CPNs to develop their roles in managing crises in the primary care setting is now, as we have discussed, of a very different kind to that in which the practice developments we have described were able to flourish. The contracting process has highlighted the legitimacy question. At the same time, the understanding Caplan (1964) offered, of everybody having mental health care needs and mental health being everybody's responsibility, fits less easily with late 1990s of Britain than it did with the welfarist Kennedy and Johnson administration of 1960s USA in which it arose. The contemporary British mental health policy of prioritising the severely mentally ill implicitly suggests that they are qualitatively different to everybody else. They are held to be in need of management and supervision rather than to be the victims of personal crisis for which they require support. Services are to be targeted, with these latter closely defined needs to be met, rather than a comprehensive range of needs, involving an overview of social and medical issues, as Caplan proposed. In this context, preventive mental health work and mental health promotion have taken on a new meaning. Seemingly, prevention in the late 1990s entails the risk assessment of the severely mentally ill's potential to harm the public or themselves.

Given the key attributes that CPNs possess, of being able to assess both clinical and social aspects of mental health crises in the community, it is perhaps up to them to be able to demonstrate that their work is effective in this area, if they are to be able to further develop it against the difficult policy context we have referred to. As has been shown in the earlier chapters by Pilgrim, Matthews, and Hogan and Orme, effectiveness, and the related topic of evidence based practice, are issues that should be approached with caution in relation to crisis services. Whose idea of evidence and whose idea of effectiveness is at stake? CPNs as a body need to document, and bring to wider public attention, the relatively high levels of satisfaction of clients with their services, whether these clients be GPs as purchasers or patients as users. A focus on these aspects of effectiveness is crucial to their participation in the development of a mental health services framework in which crisis management does not turn out to be little more than risk assessment and surveillance.

References

Armstrong, D. (1983), 'The fabrication of the nurse-patient relationship', *Social Science and Medicine*, Vol. 17, pp. 457–60.

Atha, C. (1990), 'The role of the CPN with clients who deliberately harm themselves', in Brooker, C. (ed.), *Community Psychiatric Nursing*, Chapman and Hall, London.

Brooking, J. and Minghella, E. (1987), 'Parasuicide', *Nursing Times*, Vol. 83, No. 21, pp. 40–3.

Bune, J. (1985), 'Preventive Role', *Nursing Mirror,* Vol. 161, No. 7, p. 29.

Caplan, G. (1964), *Principles of Preventive Psychiatry*, Tavistock, London.

Carlisle, D. (1990), 'Lockerbie one year on', *Nursing Times*, Vol. 86, No. 1, pp. 54–6.

Carpenter, M. (1985), *They Still Go Marching On: A Celebration of COHSE's First 75 Years*, Confederation of Health Service Employees, London.

Carr, P.J., Butterworth, C.A. and Hodges, B.E. (1980), *Community Psychiatric Nursing: caring for the mentally ill and handicapped in the community*, Churchill Livingstone, Edinburgh.

Department of Health (1989), *Caring for People: Community Care into the Next Decade and Beyond*, HMSO, London.

Department of Health (1990), *National Health Service and Community Care Act*, HMSO, London.

Department of Health (1992), *The Health of the Nation*, HMSO, London.

Department of Health (1994a), *Working in Partnership: A collaborative approach to care. Report of the mental health nursing review team*, HMSO, London.

Department of Health (1994b), 'Introduction of Supervision Registers for Mentally Ill People from 1st April 1994', HSG(94)5, HMSO, London.

Department of Health (1995), *Mental Health (Patients in the Community) Act 1995*, HMSO, London.

Department of Health (1998), *Our Healthier Nation*, HMSO, London.

Department of Health and Social Security (1970), *Local Authority Social Services Act*, HMSO, London.

Godin, P. and Scanlon, C. (1997), 'Supervision and control: a community psychiatric nursing perspective', *Journal of Mental Health*, Vol. 6, No. 1, pp. 75–84.

Godin, P. and Wilson, I. (1986), 'Selling Skills: why do so few GPs refer patients to community psychiatric nurses?', *Nursing Times (Community Outlook)*, pp. 27–9.

Goldie, N., Pilgrim, D. and Rogers, A. (1989), *Community Mental Health Centre Policy and Practice*, Good Practices in Mental Health, London.

Gournay, K. and Brooking, J. (1994), 'Community Psychiatric Nurses in Primary Health Care', *British Journal of Psychiatry*, Vol. 165, pp. 231–8.

Hendon, J. (1984), 'Liaising with the community', *Nursing Mirror*, Vol. 158, No. 22, pp. vii–viii.

Higgins, P. (1984), 'Mental Health Education', *Nursing Mirror*, Vol. 159, No. 19, pp. 28–9.

Hunter, P. (1974), 'Community Psychiatric Nursing in Britain: an historical review', *International Journal of Nursing Studies*, Vol. 11, pp. 223–33.

Lee, H. (1990), 'Out-of-hours Work by CPNs', in Brooker, C. (ed.), *Community Psychiatric Nursing: a Research Perspective*, Chapman and Hall, London.

Leopoldt, H. (1979), 'Community Psychiatric Nursing–2', *Nursing Times*, Vol. 75, No. 14, pp. 57–9.

Lindeman, E. (1944), 'Symptomatology and management of acute grief', *American Journal of Psychiatry*, Vol. 101, p. 101.

Lomax, M. (1921), *Experiences of an Asylum Doctor, with suggestions for Asylum and Lunacy Law Reform*, George Allen and Unwin, London.

McDonald, D.J. (1972), 'Psychiatric Nursing in the Community', *Nursing Times*, Vol. 68, No. 3, pp. 80–3.

McFayden, J. and Vincent, M. (1998), 'A reappraisal of community mental health nursing', *Mental Health Nursing*, Vol. 18, No. 4, pp. 19–23.

May, A.R. (1965), 'The Psychiatric Nurse in the Community', *Nursing Mirror*, Vol. 121, No. 3156, pp. 409–10.

Ministry of Health (1962), *A Hospital Plan for England and Wales, Cmnd. 1604*, HMSO, London.

Ministry of Health, Labour and Pensions Inter-Departmental Committee (1968), *Report of the Committee on Local Authority and Allied Personal Services (Seebohm Report)*, HMSO, London.

Moore, S. (1964), 'Mental Nursing in the Community', *Nursing Times*, Vol. 60, No. 15, pp. 467–70.

Morrall, P. (1995), 'Clinical Autonomy and the Community Psychiatric Nurse', *Mental Health Nursing*, Vol. 15, No. 2, pp. 16–19.

Morrall, P. (1998), *Mental Health Nursing and Social Control*, Whurr, London.

Nolan, P. (1993), *A History of Mental Health Nursing*, Chapman and Hall, London.

Onyett, S., Heppleston, T. and Bushnell, D. (1994), 'A National Survey of Community Mental Health Teams: Team Structure and Process', *Journal of Mental Health*, Vol. 3, No. 2, pp. 175–94.

Parnell, J.W. (1974), 'Psychiatric Nursing in the Community', *Queen's Nursing Journal*, Vol. 27, No. 2, pp. 36–8.

Patmore, C. and Weaver, T. (1991), 'Missing the CMHC Bus', *Nursing Times*, Vol. 87, No. 17, pp. 32–4.

Pollock, L. (1989), *Community Psychiatric Nursing – Myth and the Reality*, Scutari Press, London.

Psychiatric Nursing Today and Tomorrow (1968), *Report of the Joint Sub-Committee of Standing Mental Health and Standing Nursing Advisory Committees*, HMSO, London.

Pullen, I. and Gilbert, M.A. (1979), 'When crisis hits the home …', *Nursing Mirror*, Vol. 149, No. 14, pp. 30–2.

Robertson, H. and Scott, D. (1985), 'Community Psychiatric Nursing: a survey of patients and problems', *Journal of the Royal College of General Practitioners*, Vol. 35, pp. 130–2.

Rogers, A. and Pilgrim, D. (1996), *Mental Health Policy in Britain: A Critical Introduction*, Macmillan, London.

Royal College of Nursing (1966), *Investigation into the Role of the Psychiatric Nurse in the Community*, unpublished.

Royal College of Psychiatrists (1980), 'Community Psychiatric Nursing: a discussion document', *Bulletin of the Royal College of Psychiatry*, Vol. 4, No. 8, pp. 114–18.

Sayce, L., Craig, T. and Boardman, A.P. (1991), 'The development of Community Mental Health Centres in the U.K.', *Social Psychiatry and Psychiatric Epidemiology*, Vol. 26, pp. 14–20.

Sharpe, D. (1975), 'Role of the Community Psychiatric Nurse', *Nursing Mirror*, Vol. 141, No. 16, pp. 60–62.

Simmons, S. and Brooker, C. (1986), *Community Psychiatric Nursing: A social perspective*, Heinmann, London.

Skidmore, D. (1986), 'The Effectiveness of Community Psychiatric Nursing Teams Base Location', in Brooking, J. (ed.), *Psychiatric Nursing Research*, Wiley, Chichester.

Sladden, S. (1979), *Psychiatric Nursing in the Community: A Study of Working Situation*, Churchill Livingstone, Edinburgh.

Stobie, G. and Hopkins (1972), 'Crisis Intervention 1 and 2: A Psychiatric Community Nurse in Rural Area', *Nursing Times*, Vol. 68, No. 43, pp. 165–72.

Storer, D., Whitworth, R. and Atha, C. (1987), 'Community Psychiatric Intervention in an Accident and Emergency department: a clinical pilot study', *Journal of Advanced Nursing*, Vol. 12, pp. 215–22.

Warren, J. (1971), 'Long-acting Phenothiazine Injections given by Psychiatric Nurses in the Community', *Nursing Times*, Vol. 67, No. 36, pp. 141–3.

White, E. (1986), 'Factors Influencing GPs to Refer Patients to CPNs', in Brooking, J. (ed.), *Psychiatric Nursing Research*, Wiley, Chichester.

White, E. (1993) 'Community psychiatric nursing 1980 to 1990: a review of organisation, education and practice', in Brooker, C. and White, E. (eds), *Community Psychiatric Nursing: A Research Perspective, Volume 2*, Chapman and Hall, London.

9 Crisis Mental Health Nursing: Developments in Accident and Emergency Departments

TOM CLARKE AND CHRISTOPHER SCANLON

Introduction

The role and function of the mental health nurse within the Accident and Emergency department (A and E) has generated considerable interest within both general and mental health nursing. A growing body of literature has addressed itself to this specialist area of work, in particular to the functions of psychiatric liaison, consultation, assessment, and care planning and management. The government's most recent review of mental health nursing regarded developments in liaison nursing, across a range of non-psychiatric settings, as an important area for advanced nursing practice (Department of Health – DoH, 1994). Significantly, perhaps, the review gave no formal consideration to the specific scope of practice, qualifications or organisational requirements. In the same year, however, the Royal College of Psychiatry's Liaison Psychiatry Special Interest Group did publish the UK's first examination of the need for, as well as the scope and configuration of, liaison psychiatry services (Benjamin et al., 1994).

The role of the psychiatric nurse practising in the A and E setting is generally described in terms of two functions: the management of psychiatric emergencies presenting to A and E and liaison or consultation with hospital and community-based colleagues. The concepts such descriptions borrow from – the psychiatric emergency and liaison psychiatry – do not seem entirely appropriate when one considers the function of the mental health nurse in A and E as represented in the literature and there is confusion evident in the way different terms are used interchangeably, particularly the terms 'liaison' and 'consultation'. Although problematic, the convention has been to group such roles under the heading of liaison psychiatry and this is adopted here.

In this chapter we will consider a number of trends in health service policy

121

and provision which have influenced the development of mental health nursing in non-psychiatric settings – in particular, the Accident and Emergency department (A and E). Following a brief overview of the mental health policy arena, the underlying concepts informing the development of liaison psychiatry and mental health nursing in the UK are discussed before the role of the mental health nurse in A and E is considered.

The Mental Health Arena

Since the 1970s, the roles of the state, of markets and of citizenship have all been challenged, leading to fundamental changes in the organisation and delivery of health services (Taylor-Gooby and Lawson, 1993). Latterly, the responsibility for commissioning patient services to meet the health care needs of local populations has come to rest with unitary health authorities and General Practitioners. This devolution of responsibility from the national to a local level has been central in the evolution of a primary-care led NHS (NHSME, 1993a; NHSE, 1994). Arguably, however, it is in the field of mental health that these fundamental changes are most apparent and have been the most far-reaching (Ham, 1992).

In recent years, social policy towards mental health has been concerned with the processes of deinstitutionalisation and decarceration. Changing attitudes in society towards the care and treatment of the mentally ill, central policy initiatives and peripheral service developments, together with ideological and economic reasons have all contributed to a culture of change (Turner, 1987; Small, 1989; Baggott, 1994; also see Godin and Scanlon, this volume). The culture of change, which continues to unfold around us, has presented considerable challenges to the professional status and the practice of mental health nursing and of psychiatry. The demise of the institution and the processes of normalisation and integration, which underpin the philosophy of community care, has demanded that both professional groups radically reconsider their respective roles. The loss of their traditional institutional roles has led commentators to consider subsequent developments in both nursing and psychiatric practice from the perspective of both groups attempts to re-establish themselves as the main actors in the production and delivery of mental health services (Nolan, 1993). Whilst the general hospital remains the central institution for the production and delivery of medical health care, the rhetoric of government policy is that care in the community is the principal means of service response to mental illness (Pilgrim and Rogers, 1993).

In the UK, the policies of deinstitutionalisation and decarceration were accompanied by the recommendation that psychiatric services be established within district general hospitals (DHSS, 1962; DHSS, 1975). These were envisaged as including in-patient, day-patient and out-patient facilities. While policy is centrally generated, the level of provision of services depends, in the main, on locally-based decisions. It is for this reason that, as Freeman (1993), points out, there is an enormous variability in the level of provision of mental health services. Three decades on from the original recommendations the provision of psychiatric services within district general hospitals (DGHs) remains partial and patchy. Central government's stringent restrictions on capital spending, and promotion of the 'private finance initiative' to fund new estate developments, have been implicated in the failure to have progressed further with the DGH plan. At the same time, subsequent mental health policy developments could be argued to have diverted attention and resources to other areas.

Certainly, mental health services, together with services for the elderly and services for those with physical and learning difficulties, have traditionally failed to secure an adequate share of the public purse (Ham, 1992). It is unlikely that few if any district psychiatry services have adequate staffing levels to provide the extra staff resources required for a dedicated liaison service (Kessel, 1996). Destructive professional rivalries, particularly within the mental health field, have also been implicated in the failure to achieve policy objectives (Martin, 1984; Stuart and Sundeen, 1991; Lloyd, 1995; The Sainsbury Centre, 1997). This last point, while hardly unfounded, is often made in such a way that precludes thinking about the creative possibilities presented by professional rivalries. It also fails to appreciate the negative and divisive impact of the conflicting demands placed on mental health professionals to organise and deliver comprehensive community-based mental health services in a primary-care led NHS. Despite the variations in the development of psychiatric services within DGHs, one widespread associated development is the growing interest in the mental health needs of the physically ill in-patient – what has come to be referred to under the rubric 'liaison psychiatry' (DoH, 1994; RCP/RCPsych, 1995). As with the general psychiatric services the pace and extent of the development of liaison psychiatry varies considerably from one place to the next.

Liaison

The collaborative nature implied by the term *liaison* stems from a shared interest in the psychosomatic aspects of medicine between general and specialist psychiatric physicians, in Europe and North America. This led to the development of dedicated facilities within general hospital settings in the US and to specialist services for people with psychosomatic disorders elsewhere in Europe (Lipowski, 1967; Wolff et al., 1990; Roberts and Taylor, 1997). In the UK, such developments have been slow to materialise and the scope of liaison psychiatry – originally the psychological care of patients with physical illnesses – has been extended to include responses to the mental health needs of medical patients with a known or suspected mental illness (Wolff et al., 1990; Benjamin et al., 1994). Two distinct but overlapping bodies of work have heavily influenced the concept of liaison mental health nursing in the UK. The first is the 'consultation' model developed by Caplan (1970) and the second is the 'liaison' model developed by Lipowski (1981).

In the first model, Caplan (1970) presents an independent mental health nurse specialist (the consultant) who is consulted to assist in solving a work-related problem. Although a range of models of consultation have been developed which might be subsumed under the heading 'organisational consultancy' (see, for example, Hansen et al., 1990), the focus here is confined to the type of consultation typically found in medical and nursing practice in the UK. In this model, the consultee may, for example, be a hospital physician concerned about some aspect of a patient's mental health and who requests a psychiatric assessment. On completion of the consultation, in this case, a psychiatric assessment, the consultant withdraws and has no further responsibility for the patient. This is the most common scenario encountered in the general hospital.

In the second model, Lipowski (1981) presents an essentially medically-orientated model where the mental health nurse is not represented as an independent consultant, but is part of a multi-disciplinary liaison team. Less usual, and generally only where specialist liaison nursing is well-established, are direct nurse-to-nurse requests and referrals. Such activity does not necessarily involve direct contact with a patient, and the consultant may impart advice, teach, or otherwise provide support – for example, through supervision in particular cases. Lipowski also makes much use of the term 'consultation', but this is to be differentiated from Caplan's use of the term. Lipowski's concept of consultation is qualified by an emphasis on 'collaboration' between the mental health specialists comprising the liaison team and their non-psychiatric colleagues. Through cultivating enabling inter-professional relationships, joint working is promoted and the liaison team or team member stays involved with the on-going care of the patient.

Criticism has been levied at operational accounts of liaison services for failing to distinguish between the differing models (Tunmore and Thomas, 1992). Ryrie et al. (1997) also note the resultant confusion evident in the literature and query the extent to which practitioners have comprehended the dual concepts of liaison and consultation. However, while a consultation-style service, mainly provided by psychiatrists, prevails in the UK (Lloyd, 1995) Egan-Morriss and her colleagues (1994) consider that little is as yet known about how mental health nurses can work with colleagues and patients in non-psychiatric settings and that innovative approaches remain to be developed.

Function and Role in Liaison

An extensive range of clinical psychiatric problems are encountered in the general hospital or other non-psychiatric health-care setting which differ from those more commonly seen in the psychiatric health-care setting (Lloyd, 1995). Tunmore (1994) identifies two main client groups to whom liaison mental health nurses provide interventions. The first group are physically ill people who may be experiencing emotional or psychological distress, for example in the face of a major or life-threatening illness. The second group comprises those with somatic manifestations of emotional or psychological distress. For such people the physical symptoms they experience are rooted not in a medical condition but have their origins in deep unresolved personal and interpersonal conflicts.

Interventions available to the liaison mental health nurse will depend on the individual's skills and qualifications. These could include short-term specific psychological interventions, for example anxiety-management techniques, and the provision of recognised psychological therapies, for example psychotherapy (Tunmore, 1990; Egan-Morriss et al., 1994). The role of the liaison mental health nurse has been described as 'bridging the gap' between a patient's needs and the ability of the general nurse to manage psychological care (Tunmore, 1990). Such a model implies a high degree of clinical and interpersonal skills on the part of the liaison nurse and a willingness by both the liaison and general nurse to collaborate in achieving optimum care for their patient. Elsewhere, Tunmore and Thomas, (1992) have described differing models of consultation liaison mental health nursing focusing on the twin concepts of liaison and consultation. Essentially, the practice of liaison is defined as the sum of the parts constituting the potential relationship in caring for the patient. On the other hand, the practice of consultation is defined as the sum of the parts constituting the potential relationship with medical or surgical colleagues (see Table 9.1 below).

Table 9.1   Comparative characteristics of liaison and consultation in mental health nursing

Liaison – direct care	Consultation – indirect care
• Referral to multi-disciplinary team	• Request to specialist mental health practitioner
• Psychosocial assessment	• Problem identification

• Negotiated careplan	• Problem solution
	  − intervention (e.g.psychosocial assessment)
	  − advice
	  − teaching
	  − support
	  − supervision

• Therapeutic intervention or referral to appropriate agency	
• Evaluation	
• On-going	• Time limited

The nursing practice of liaison, therefore, comprises psychosocial assessment, the negotiation of a careplan, and the implementation and evaluation of that careplan. Specific therapeutic interventions may be carried out by the practitioner or referral made to an appropriate agency or specialist. The nursing practice of consultation is defined as including teaching, advice giving and support to non-psychiatric colleagues caring for the patient without the practitioner necessarily being directly involved with the patient (Tunmore, 1990; Stuart and Sundeen, 1991; Tunmore and Thomas, 1992; Egan-Morriss et al., 1994; Ryrie et al., 1997). The term liaison mental health, however, has increasingly come to refer to the management of so-called psychiatric emergencies, especially within Accident and Emergency departments (Edgeley and Rowell, 1994). This (mis-) appropriation of the term 'liaison' is evident in much of the literature to the degree that the promotion of the psychological care of patients with physical illness appears to have been eclipsed by the current emphasis on providing services to patients who present at A and E, particularly as a result of having self-harmed.

Accident and Emergency Mental Health Nursing

A and E medicine is one of the more recent medical specialities to emerge in industrialised countries. In part, its emergence has been tied to that of dissatisfaction with the standards of its predecessor, the Casualty or Emergency Receiving Room, and in part with the aims of senior doctors who did not have consultant status to have their speciality recognised and consultants appointed (Rutherford, 1989).

A distinguishing characteristic of the A and E department is that it is the only 24 hour a day open access medical facility. As a result anyone can, and often does, wander in, presenting A and E staff with a range of complex non-medical personal and social problems to deal with. The various agencies including the police, social services and general practice are also perceived at times as bringing or referring patients with primarily non-medical problems (Redmond, 1989; Rutherford, 1989). The A and E department also retains a significant role in the provision of emergency psychiatric services despite developments in community mental health care, especially at night when alternative specialist provision is likely to be closed (Atha et al., 1989a; Johnson and Thornicroft, 1994).

Definitions of the psychiatric emergency abound and can appear tautological. In relation to the A and E setting it would seem that the term is often used to refer to almost any situation the mental health professional might encounter (Pisarcik, 1981; Merker, 1986; Redmond, 1989). For example, Faumann and Faumann (1981) define a psychiatric emergency as an 'alteration in behaviour, mood, or thought which the patient, a friend, relative or professional feels requires immediate medical attention'. In his treatment of the subject Clark (1982) concludes that the analogy with the medical emergency is misleading and that the reasons for presentation are often associated with seeking solutions for a particular problem in the community, rather than seeking a specific psychiatric requirement.

Contemporary Influences

Currently, there is a focus on self-harm by liaison services within A and E and this can be traced back to 1968 when the then Ministry of Health recommended that all patients admitted to hospital following an act of self-harm be assessed by a psychiatrist (Loveridge et al., 1997). However, since then the trend has generally been for fewer adults to receive a psychiatric assessment.

Additionally, there is some evidence that younger persons who self-harm are also being discharged from A and E without a psychiatric assessment – despite recommendations to the contrary (Owens, 1990; O'Dwyer et al., 1991).

In the UK, deliberate self-harm is the most common reason for acute medical admission of women to hospital, and is second only to ischaemic heart disease for the admission of men. Estimates have put the figure for repeated acts as high as 50 per cent in some places (Hawton and Catalan, 1987; Evans et al., 1996). The epidemiology of self-harm is also relevant to the prevention of suicide. Reports have shown an increased risk of death from suicide in individuals who have made previous suicide attempts and/or have previously harmed themselves. It is estimated that one per cent of individuals who attend hospital having harmed themselves die from suicide within a year of the original act, and some three per cent during the following five years (Hawton and Fagg, 1988). Follow-up studies have indicated that up to 14 per cent of all those who have made a non-fatal attempt will eventually die from suicide (Diekstra, 1992). In view of this and the fact that up to a quarter of people who make suicide attempts have attended hospital in the previous year, the Royal College of Psychiatrists has called for improved services within A and E to this population. Such services are argued as having a significant contribution to make to achieving the relevant Health of the Nation targets (RCPsych, 1994). While the significance of self-harm as a predictor of suicide is difficult to determine, it remains the case that evidence of self-harm is the strongest indicator of risk available to the clinician (Wolff et al., 1990; Diekstra, 1992). An important and realistic goal therefore in the management of self-harm is to reduce repetition.

Although there has been much effort, there is at present limited firm evidence that availability of a particular mix of specialist services reduces repetition (Moller, 1989). Even if there were clearly defined programs available, there would still be the problem that many patients are discharged without adequate assessment or planned follow-up. Despite the development of nursing triage in A and E (the process of classifying patients according to priority for attention, by means of rapid assessment and the initiation of treatment procedures where necessary), it remains the case that a proportion of A and E self-harm patients discharge themselves from hospital before a psychiatric assessment can be carried out and/or a care plan formulated (Edgeley and Rowell, 1994).

It is possible then, that the present emphasis on self-harm reflects in part the response by the health services to the Health of the Nation targets where a priority is a reduction in suicide rates (DoH, 1991). Subsequently, it has been widely publicised that those who self-harm are at a far greater risk of killing themselves within the following year than the general population (NHSME, 1993b; RCPscyh, 1994). While the effectiveness of interventions to prevent suicide continues to be found wanting self-harm, as one of the commonest reasons for admission to hospital, presents the health services with an important opportunity for intervention (Gunnell and Frankel, 1994; Hawton and James, 1995). As noted above, A and E is the main resource for out-of-hours emergency psychiatric referrals, and as such is often required to provide for the emergency management of the severely mentally ill (Johnson and Thornicroft, 1994). This is another group for whom the risk of suicide is far greater than in the general population and who have been made a priority in setting the Health of the Nation targets (DoH, 1991).

In any intervention the assessment of risk, both of repeating the self-harm and of completing suicide, as well as the risk presented to others, is a primary task which raises the question of who is appropriately qualified and skilled to do the intervening. A number of studies support the view that specifically trained nurses are effective assessors of risk and of psychiatric morbidity when compared with psychiatrists (Catalan et al., 1980; Brooking and Minghella, 1987). The broad knowledge base of nurses, their competence in psychosocial assessment, as well as their holistic philosophical approach, have been cited as effective in bridging the psychiatric, medical and social aspects of care required in the A and E setting (Pisarcik, 1981; Merker, 1986; Brooking and Minghella, 1987).

The promotion of strategies for suicide prevention in respect of those who self-harm and the seriously mentally ill has led to a growing number of mental health nurses developing roles and services within A and E, of which risk-assessment is only part, albeit a major part.

Function and Role in A and E

A review of the function of mental health services in A and E indicates a number of common features although the level of resources in terms of personnel may vary considerably. Generally, such services are provided by mental health nurses. Additional support may be provided by an on-call psychiatric registrar and services are usually overseen by a Consultant Psychiatrist (Loveridge, 1997; Watts, 1997). Resource limitations mean that 24 hour provision cannot be provided although some attempts have been made to deploy resources at times of greatest perceived need, for example in the evenings and at weekends.

The patient population is varied and in addition to those who self harm and those with a psychiatric illness, the nurse will also encounter people presenting with psychosomatic disorders, victims of assault, people at various stages of intoxication as well as those with drug and alcohol problems, those who are homeless and others experiencing a range of life crises (Merker, 1986; Ryrie et al., 1997). As with the liaison mental health model previously described, practitioners generally do not have dedicated facilities available to them and utilise what is available within the setting at the time to see a patient; be this the bedside, an interview room, the waiting-room or the relatives room (Loveridge et al., 1997). Following triage, or where this is required following medical assessment/treatment, the patient is referred to the mental health nurse for psychosocial assessment (Roberts and Taylor, 1997). In some instances, for example where a psychotic illness is suspected, the psychiatrist may see the patient first. In this scenario, the role of the nurse is not as the primary assessor but is to deliver an appropriate intervention to those patients subsequently passed on by the psychiatrist.

Unlike the liaison mental health model described previously, the intervention stage here will rarely involve the provision of recognised psychological therapies. A number of patients may require specific brief psychological interventions, for example, those presenting with symptoms of panic disorder and the relatives of a patient who has died. Often the nurse is required to impart health promotion advice, for example in the case of problem drinking or drug abuse. Advocacy is often cited as an important part of the role and the nurse may represent the patient in dealings with other agencies, for example by telephoning housing and social security services (Watts, 1997). Referral on to appropriate services and agencies through which, for example, arrangements can be made for further psychiatric assessment, is a significant function of the mental health nurse's role. This may necessitate contacting other NHS trusts when the patient does not live within the receiving A and E Trust's catchment area and occasionally escorting such patients (Roberts and Taylor, 1997).

Assessment, brief psychological interventions, advocacy and referral comprise the main activities of the mental health nurse in A and E. The current emphasis on responding to the needs of those who have self-harmed means that this group constitute the greater part of those seen. In addition, Atha et al. (1989b) emphasise the importance of the role as a resource for A and E staff embracing information sharing, e.g. on psychiatric facilities locally, liaison between psychiatric teams and the A and E department, education and staff support, including supervision. Specialist services have also been developed in some centres aimed at specific subgroups of attendees at A and E, for example, those who self-harm and those who present for psychological reasons (Brooking and Minghella, 1987; Atha et al., 1989b). In this context, eligible patients are offered time-limited 'crisis counselling' either in their own homes or in an out-patient clinic.

Research and Evaluation

The introduction of a mixed-economy into health care has led to increased demands for the systematic assessment of services (Phillips et al., 1994). Yet, the resultant growing research base has produced little impact on the design of services or treatments – the contribution of skill and knowledge from research findings to the field being negligible (Parry, 1994).

   Although the reasons for this are varied and complex , a major factor is the dynamic and situated nature of notions of health and ill-health giving rise to a multiplicity of views about 'health', 'illness' and 'disease'. Consequently, the multiple and complex ways in which such views are used discursively inform and shape every action within health service settings, whether treatment, cure, care, prevention or health care promotion (Curtis and Taket, 1996).

   This view is encapsulated in Klein's (1982) description of the health policy arena as characterised by complexity, heterogeneity, uncertainty and ambiguity. Complexity is evident in the wide range of occupations involved in providing services; heterogeneity in the variety of services provided; uncertainty in the absence of a clear relationship between inputs and outputs; and ambiguity in the meaning of the information which is available. Given these factors, Klein concluded that performance evaluation is most usefully seem as a process of argument. While Klein's description is all too familiar it does go some way to explaining why good research is so difficult to achieve and has such limited impact. Despite this, it remains the case that there is a clear need to establish a culture of service-led research aimed at improving the quality of patient care and which will inform mental health nursing (Brooking, 1985; DoH, 1994).

   Much of the research work currently undertaken with patients presenting at A and E is addressed to those who self-harm with an emphasis on broad interventions to heterogeneous groups. The experiences of researchers in this area could prove invaluable to liaison mental health nurse researchers. In particular, the heterogeneity of the study populations has been posited as an important explanation for the lack of positive outcomes in such work (Van der Sande et al., 1997). One suggestion has been that future studies should address homogenous subgroups of patients sharing similar problems related to self-harm episodes (ibid.). Likewise, liaison mental health nurses when designing research and evaluation protocols for the A and E setting might consider smaller homogenous subgroups of patients presenting with similar problems, as well as the general population encountered. With patients who self-harm this could involve, for example, regarding patients with a serious mental illness or with a history of multiple presentations as distinct patient groupings.

Discussion

Considerable confusion surrounds the terminology used to describe the function and role of mental health nursing in non-psychiatric settings which requires further clarification (Tunmore and Thomas 1992; Ryrie et al., 1997). As these are relatively recent developments in the UK and not widely established, such clarification may be some way off and will depend on the future direction(s) forged by nurse practitioners and their medical colleagues. It may be that the language used serves the purpose of legitimisation of a contested role by a profession uncertain of its direction, rather than adequately describes that role. At the same time, as in any emergent field, a concomitant of developing practice is developing a language to construct and convey that practice with all the possibilities this presents for confusion.

From the literature, Lipowski's (1981) concept of consultation is regarded as the cornerstone of much of what is referred to as liaison mental health work. Consultation in this context requires collaboration and is a two way process. The range and nature of tasks implicit in this two-way process has been operationalised in the 'collaborative' model developed by Dunn (1989). The two parties – the mental health nurse and the A and E staff team are each regarded as constituting a partnership where each has specific contributions to make. The mental health nurse contributes support, expert knowledge, skills and objectivity while the A and E staff team provide the essential information, medical knowledge and skills and the necessary resources. In this respect we suggest that the view of liaison mental health nursing as a straightforward development of the traditional role of the mental health nurse is too narrow. The present and future roles of practitioners depends as much on the capacity of non-psychiatric colleagues to incorporate a psychosocial perspective into their practice as on initiatives by mental health nurses.

The level of willingness of Consultant Physicians and Psychiatrists to accept and to encourage nurse to nurse referrals will also influence the extent to which the role of senior nurse practitioner can develop. Within the UK, the traditional medical model does not contemplate such a referral route and the liaison mental health nurse will likely have to lobby hard to cultivate a more enabling professional climate (Egan-Morriss et al., 1994). Amongst current developments, the emphasis on developing suicide strategies may wane if disillusionment with their effectiveness sets in. This might jeopardise the on-going provision of A and E based interventions and so limit the opportunities for mental health nurses to develop services in this area.

The relatively low incidence of mental illness in those seen and the doubtful but widespread classification of cases as 'psychiatric emergencies' raises a number of problematic issues regarding the present and future provision of mental health services within the A and E setting (Clark, 1982; Loveridge et al., 1997). In particular, an enduring criticism of psychiatry generally has been its role in social control through the medicalisation of behaviours deemed deviant (Pilgrim and Rogers, 1993). There is a perceived risk in the present context, if not already a reality, of applying an inappropriate medical model to essentially personal and social problems which may deflect from the need for appropriate political debate and action (Busfield, 1980; Hopton, 1997). A related issue is the extent to which mental health nurses can or should be involved in promoting mental health as opposed to a more traditional model of the care and treatment of mental ill-health (Pavis et al., 1998).

As previously noted, there is a prevailing political concern that the needs of the seriously mentally ill continue to be neglected and that the expansion of the role of the mental health nurse into other areas can only serve to exacerbate this. The future direction of mental health nursing continues to be debated with a powerful lobby calling for changes in training and a narrower focus of practice emphasising the care of those with a serious and enduring mental illness (Gournay and Beadsmoore, 1995; Gournay and Brooking, 1994; The Sainsbury Centre, 1997). At the same time, it is likely that the A and E department will continue to be a focus for emergency psychiatric referrals, especially out of hours referrals. In this respect, mental health nurses have much to offer in the development of a network of accessible and responsive services to the mentally ill.

The recent English version of the White Paper *The New NHS: Modern, Dependable* proposes to end the internal market and establish Primary Care Groups (PGPs) headed by General Practitioners in partnership with local health authorities and social service departments. Community-based nurses are also envisaged as having a leading role to play in the PGPs and are to be actively involved in the commissioning of NHS services (DoH, 1997). No specific provision is made for mental health services and how they will fare under the new proposals remains to be seen. Bearing in mind the political objectives referred to earlier it seems unlikely that creative developments such as liaison mental health nursing will have a high priority and the specialism could well remain the preserve of the interested few.

Of course, the calls for a reappraisal of the education and role mental health nursing also present possibilities for practitioners to influence subsequent developments. Alliances with non-psychiatric colleagues also present creative possibilities. In the UK at least, this would have to be achieved in a professional climate which has been described as characterised by a lack of mutual support and co-operation (Nolan, 1993). Obstacles will no doubt be encountered, but the recent moves to establish a faculty of A and E nursing (Crouch and Jones, 1997; Garbett, 1998) indicate one sphere where formal alliances might prove fruitful – for example, if mental health nurses practising in A and E were to pursue associate membership should efforts to establish a faculty come to fruition.

References

Atha, C., Salkovskis, P. and Storer, D. (1989a), 'More Questions Than Answers', *Nursing Times*, Vol. 85, No. 15, pp. 28–31.

Atha, C., Salkovskis, P. and Storer, D. (1989b), 'Problem-Solving Treatment', *Nursing Times*, Vol. 85, No. 17, pp. 45–7.

Baggott, R. (1994), *Health and Health Care in Britain*, St. Martin's Press, London.

Benjamin, S., House, A. and Jenkins, P. (eds) (1994), *Liaison Psychiatry: Defining Needs and Planning Services*, Gaskell, London.

Brooking, J.I. (1985), 'Advanced Psychiatric Nursing Education in Britain', *Journal of Advanced Nursing*, Vol. 10, pp. 445–68.

Brooking, J.I. and Minghella, E. (1987), 'Parasuicide', *Nursing Times*, Vol. 83, No. 21, pp. 40–3.

Busfield, J. (1996), 'Professionals, the State and the Development of Mental Health Policy', in Heller, T. et al. (eds), *Mental Health Matters: A Reader*, Macmillan, in association with the Open University, London.

Caplan, G. (1970), *The Theory and Practice of Mental Health Consultation*, Tavistock, London.

Catalan, J., Marsack, P., Hawton, K.E., Whitwell, D., Fagg, J. and Bancroft, J.H.J. (1980), 'Comparison of Doctors and Nurses in the Assessment of Deliberate Self-Poisoning Patients', *Psychological Medicine*, Vol. 10, pp. 483–92.

Clark, I. (1982), 'Psychiatric Emergency: Concepts and Problems of Organisational Structure', *Sociology of Health and Illness*, Vol. 4, No. 1, pp. 75–85.

Crouch, R. and Jones, G. (1997), 'Towards a Faculty of Emergency Nursing: Planning for the Future', *Emergency Nurse*, Vol. 5, No. 6, pp. 12–15.

Curtis, S. and Taket, A. (1996), *Health and Societies. Changing Perspectives*, Arnold, London.

Department of Health (DoH) (1991), *The Health of the Nation*, HMSO, London.

Department of Health (DoH) (1994), *Working in Partnership: A Collaborative Approach to Care*, HMSO, London.

Department of Health (DoH) (1997), *The New NHS: Modern, Dependable*, HMSO, London.

Department of Health and Social Security (DHSS) (1962), *Hospital Plan for England and Wales*, HMSO, London.

Department of Health and Social Security (DHSS) (1975), *Better Services for the Mentally Ill*, HMSO, London.

Diekstra, R.F.W. (1992), 'Epidemiology of Suicide: Aspects of Definition, Classification and Preventative Policies', in Crepet, P., Ferrari, G., Platt, S. and Bellini, M. (eds), *Suicidal Behaviour in Europe – Recent Research Findings*, John Libbey, Rome.

Dunn, J. (1989), 'Psychiatric Emergencies in the Community Emergency Room', *Journal of Nursing Administration*, Vol. 19, No. 10, pp. 36–40.

Edgeley, S.P. and Rowell, D.W. (1994), 'Liaison Psychiatry in A and E', in Sbaih, L. (ed), *Issues in Accident and Emergency Nursing*, Chapman and Hall, London.

Egan-Morriss, E., Morriss, R. and House, A. (1994), 'The Role of the Nurse in Consultation-Liaison Psychiatry', in Benjamin, S., House, A. and Jenkins, P. (eds), *Liaison Psychiatry: Defining Needs and Planning Services*, Gaskell, London.

Evans, J., Platts, H. and Liebenau, A. (1996), 'Impulsiveness and Deliberate Self-Harm: A Comparison of "First-timers" and "Repeaters"', *Acta Psychiatrica Scandinavica*, Vol. 93, pp. 378–80.

Faumann, B.J. and Faumann, M.A. (1981), *Emergency Psychiatry for the House Officer*, Williams and Wilkins, Baltimore.

Freeman, H. (1993), 'The History of British Community Psychiatry', in Dean, C. and Freeman, H., *Community Mental Health Care International Perspectives on Making it Happen*, Gaskell and the Centre for Mental Health Services Development, London.

Garbett, R. (1997), 'Clear Passage to A and E', *Nursing Times*, Vol. 93, No. 41, p. 18.

Gerson, S. and Bassuk, E. (1980), 'Psychiatric Emergencies: An Overview', *American Journal of Psychiatry*, Vol. 137, No. 1, pp. 1–11.

Gournay, K. and Beadsmoore, A. (1995), 'The Report of the Clinical Standards Advisory Group: Standards for People with Schizophrenia in the UK and Implications for Mental Health Nursing', *Journal of Psychiatric and Mental Health Nursing*, Vol. 2, pp. 359–64.

Gournay, K.J.M. and Brooking, J.I. (1994), 'The Community Psychiatric Nurse in Primary Care: An Outcome Study', *British Journal of Psychiatry*, Vol. 165, pp. 231–8.

Gunnell, D. and Frankel, S. (1994), 'Prevention of Suicide: Aspirations and Evidence', *British Medical Journal*, Vol. 308, pp. 1227–33.

Ham, C. (1992), *Health Policy in Britain*, Macmillan, Basingstoke.

Hansen, J., Himes, B. and Meier, S. (1990), *Consultation, Concepts and Practice*, Prentice Hall, Cambridge.

Hawton, K. and Catalan, J. (1987), *Attempted Suicide: A Practical Guide to its Nature and Management*, Oxford University Press, Oxford.

Hawton, K. and Fagg, J. (1988), 'Suicide, and Other Causes of Death, Following Attempted Suicide', *British Journal of Psychiatry*, Vol. 152, pp. 359–66.

Hawton, K. and Fagg, J. (1992), 'Trends in Deliberate Self-Poisoning and Self-Injury in Oxford, 1976-90', *British Medical Journal*, Vol. 304, pp. 1409–11.

Hawton, K. and James, R. (1995), 'General Hospital Services for Attempted Suicide Patients: A Survey in One Region', *Health Trends*, Vol. 27, pp. 18–21.

Hopton, J. (1997), 'Towards a Critical Theory of Mental Health Nursing', *Journal of Advanced Nursing*, Vol. 25, pp. 492–500.

Johnson, S. and Thornicroft, G. (1994), 'General Medical Services-Accident and Emergency Departments', in Jenkins, R. (ed.), *The Prevention of Suicide*, HMSO, London.

Jones, C. and Hall, G. (1994), 'The Moral Problems Involved in the Concept of Patient Triage in the A and E Department', in Sbaih, L. (ed.), op. cit.

Kessel, N. (1996), 'Should we buy Liaison Psychiatry?', *Journal of the Royal Society of Medicine*, Vol. 89, No. 9, pp. 481–2.

Klein, R. (1983), *The Politics of the NHS*, Longman, London.

Lipowski, Z.J. (1967), 'Review of Consultation Psychiatry and Psychosomatic Medicine, 1: General Principles', *Psychosomatic Medicine*, Vol. 29, pp. 153–70.

Lipowski, Z.J. (1981), 'Liaison Psychiatry, Liaison Nursing and Behavioural Medicine', *Comprehensive Psychiatry*, Vol. 22, pp. 6554–61.

Lloyd, G.G. (1995), 'A Sense of Proportion: The Place of Psychiatry in Medicine', *Journal of the Royal Society of Medicine*, Vol. 85, pp. 563–7.

Loveridge, L., Nolan, P., Carr, N. and White, A. (1997), 'Healing Jesus', *Nursing Times*, Vol. 93, No. 30, pp. 26–30.

Martin, F.M. (1984), *Between the Acts: Community Mental Health Services*, Nuffield Provincial Hospital Trust, London.

Merker, M.S. (1986), 'Psychiatric Emergency Evaluation', *Nursing Clinics of North America*, Vol. 21, No. 3, pp. 387–96.

Moller, H.J. (1989), 'Efficacy of Different Strategies of Aftercare for Patients Who Have Attempted Suicide', *Journal of the Royal Society of Medicine*, Vol. 82, pp. 643–7.

National Health Service Executive (NHSE) (1994), *Developing NHS Purchasing and GP Fundholding*, NHSE, London.

National Health Service Management Executive (NHSME) (1993a), *Managing the New NHS*, NHSME, London.

National Health Service Management Executive (NHSME) (1993b), *Health of the Nation Key Area Handbook: Mental Illness*, NHSME, London.

Nolan, P. (1993), *A History of Mental Health Nursing*, Chapman and Hall, London.

O'Dwyer, F.G., D'Alton, A. and Pearce, J.B. (1991), 'Adolescent Self Harm Patients: Audit of Assessment in an Accident and Emergency Department', *British Medical Journal*, Vol. 303, pp. 629–30.

Owens, D. (1990), 'Self-Harm Patients not Admitted to Hospital', *Journal of the Royal College of Physicians*, Vol. 24, pp. 281–3.

Parry, G. (1994), 'Using Research to Change Practice', in Heller, T., op. cit.

Pavis, S., Secker, J., Cunningham-Burley, S. and Masters, H. (1998), 'Mental Health: What Do We Know, How Did We Find It Out And What Does It Mean For Nurses?', *Journal of Psychiatric and Mental Health Nursing*, Vol. 5, pp. 1–10.

Phillips, C., Palfrey, C. and Thomas, P. (1994), *Evaluating Health and Social Care*, Macmillan, London.

Pilgrim, D. and Rogers, A. (1993), *A Sociology of Mental Health and Illness*, Open University Press, Buckingham.

Pisarcik, G.K. (1981), 'Psychiatric Emergencies and Crisis Intervention', *Nursing Clinics of North America*, Vol. 16, No. 1, pp. 85–94.

Pritchard, C. (1995), *Suicide – The Ultimate Rejection? A Psycho-Social Study*, Open University Press, Buckingham.

Redmond, A.D. (1989), 'Psychiatric Emergencies', in Rutherford, W.H., Illingworth, R.N., Marsden, A.K., Nelson, P.G., Redmond, A.D. and Wilson, D.H. (eds), *Accident and Emergency Medicine*, Churchill Livingstone, Edinburgh.

Roberts, M. and Taylor, B. (1997), 'Emergency Action', *Nursing Times*, Vol. 93, No. 30, pp. 30–1.

Royal College of Physicians (RCP) and Royal College of Psychiatrists (RCPsych) (1995), *The Psychological Care of Medical Patients*, RCP/RCPsych, London.

Royal College of Psychiatrists (RCPsych) (1994), *The General Hospital Management of Adult Deliberate Self-Harm. A Consensus Statement on Standards for Service Provision*, Council Report CR32.

Rutherford, W.H. (1989), 'Accident and Emergency Medicine', in Rutherford, W.H., Illingworth, R.N., Marsden, A.K., Nelson, P.G., Redmond, A.D. and Wilson, D.H. (eds), *Accident and Emergency Medicine*, Churchill Livingstone, Edinburgh.

Ryrie, I., Roberts, M. and Taylor, R. (1997), 'Liaison Psychiatric Nursing in an Inner City Accident and Emergency Department', *Journal of Psychiatric and Mental Health Nursing*, Vol. 4, pp. 131–6.

Salkovskis, P., Atha, C. and Storer, D. (1989), 'Defining the Problem', *Nursing Times*, Vol. 85, No. 16, pp. 50–2.

Small, N. (1989), *Politics and Planning in the National Health Service*, Open University Press, Buckingham.

Stuart, G.W. and Sundeen, S.J. (1991), *Principles and Practice of Psychiatric Nursing*, Mosby-Year Book Inc, St. Louis.

Taylor-Gooby, P. and Lawson, R. (1993), *Markets and Managers. New Issues in the Delivery of Welfare*, Open University Press, Buckingham.

The Sainsbury Centre for Mental Health (1997), *Pulling Together. The Future Roles and Training of Mental Health Staff*, The Sainsbury Centre for Mental Health, London.

Tunmore, R. (1990), 'Setting the Pace', *Nursing Times*, Vol. 86, No. 34, pp. 29–32.

Tunmore, R. (1994), 'Encouraging Collaboration', *Nursing Times*, Vol. 90, No. 20, pp. 66–7.

Tunmore, R. and Thomas, B. (1992), 'Models of Psychiatric Consultation Liaison Nursing', *British Journal of Nursing*, Vol. 1, No. 9, pp. 447–51.

Turner, B.S. (1987), *Medical Power and Social Knowledge*, Sage, London.

Van Der Sande, R., Van Rooigen, L., Buskens, E., Allart, E., Hawton, K., Van der Graaf, Y. and Van Engeland, H. (1997), 'Intensive In-Patient and Community Intervention Versus Routine Care After Attempted Suicide', *British Journal of Psychiatry*, Vol. 171, pp. 35–41.

Watts, D. (1997), 'Brief Encounters', *Nursing Times*, Vol. 93, No. 30, pp. 28–9.

Wolff, H., Bateman, A. and Sturgeon, D. (1990), *UCH Textbook of Psychiatry – An Integrated Approach*, Duckworth, London.

10 Exemplary Crisis Services in Europe and the USA

SHULAMIT RAMON

Introduction

The issues which give rise to the need to develop mental health crisis services vary little between societies, though ways of addressing them differ greatly at times. To make sense of the different choices included in some of the examples given below it is necessary to take into account the social, cultural, political, economic and professional context which fosters and enables these choices to be made.

However, to assume that these services are 'exemplary' is rather grand, as it invites the reader to believe that they provide the definitive answer to the needs embedded in crisis work, or to the issues underlying those needs. While I would hope that the programmes to be outlined offer additional value to most of the UK services, it seems to me that the definitive answer is still out of our collective reach.

The dimensions to be considered for each programme, in respect of added value, are about the degree to which a programme has achieved the following:

- accessibility and availability;
- responsiveness;
- respect and de-stigmatisation;
- a type or types of crisis intervention; and
- effectiveness, measured in terms of reduction of suffering, the enabling function, the preventive function, and cost effectiveness.

The Netherlands

A focus on crisis intervention began to become evident earlier in the Netherlands than in most other European countries. This trend is related to the existence of community mental health facilities since 1947 in Amsterdam, but seems to be in contrast to the lack of reduction in the number of psychiatric hospitals or the number of beds in the last fifty years. De Smit (1969) comments that the country is the most densely populated in Europe, and has dealt with this fact by developing an emphasis on care and welfare. It could also be argued that the sectarian nature of the Dutch society – where 21 religious sects coexist – has been overcome as a potential source of social conflict by the high level of tolerance and by enabling welfare systems to develop alongside the religious divide. The high level of tolerance of deviancy is still in evidence today, ranging from the permission to use soft drugs publicly, and the legalisation of prostitution, to the low level of imprisonment. Likewise, the high level of spending on welfare and the professionality of the Dutch services has been maintained during recent years, while other European countries, including Britain, have cut down on welfare spending.

The health system operates through an insurance scheme, in which people pay according to income, and those without an income are covered by the state. A high proportion of welfare services is to be found in the private not-for-profit sector; this is the case for both health and social services. Most of the psychiatric hospitals are run by private companies; only 10 per cent are part of the public sector. Pertaining to mental health the Dutch user movement, and the support it has received from the government, have set an example to emulate for the rest of Europe.

Crisis intervention facilities were developed as a trouble shooting device (de Smit, 1969) in a dual sense:

- to provide intervention at all times when it is felt to be needed, around the clock; and
- to diminish the credibility gap experienced by the public towards the service capacity of the caring professions.

The Dutch approach to crisis services derives from the pioneering work carried out by Querido between 1934 and 1960 in Amsterdam. He insisted that the same professional team which provides ordinary mental health support should also offer crisis work. The first crisis centre was established in Amsterdam in 1972, with 14 beds, working around the clock. People could stay up to 72 hours. No follow up was on offer, but usually users would be referred to other services if the need for such a referral was assessed to exist. It was divided into a medical and a social component, run by professionals from psychiatry and social work. This duality was perceived as necessary to enable a comprehensive service. Often the centre provided brokerage and advocacy, for both the direct user and the community.

The centre perceived one of its main functions to be that of preventing people not simply from hospital admission, but from taking on the social and psychological role of becoming a patient. In this sense it fulfilled the functions of secondary and tertiary prevention.

De Smit argues that the centre fulfilled, in fact, five functions. These were those of:

- the consumer guide – a first-aid facility which mediates between the user and the care agencies, checking out the readiness and availability of these agencies to offer adequate responses;
- the 'test case' – of the validity of the medical model against that of a more social model;
- the trouble shooter, in terms of availability as a first port of call;
- the 'honest broker', through mediation and advocacy; and
- the 'quarter step', stopping people from entering the patient role.

Additional crisis intervention centres developed in response to the critique of psychiatric hospitals during the 1970s. Some of these offer only an out-of-hours service (Wolf, 1992). The first centre was jointly funded and run by the University Hospital and the Municipal Social Psychiatric Service. It was successful in establishing a link to the social systems, both through the local authority social services and through the connections with the criminal justice system: not a simple feat. The Dutch data provides us with information about the users of crisis services and some of the outcomes of their use.

Four main groups of users emerge:

- people who already used psychiatric services, termed 'chronic' and 'old hands';
- people using such services for the first time via a crisis service;
- people who come intoxicated from alcohol;
- people who come because of drug-induced mental illness.

Both men and women use the services in similar numbers. Younger people (aged 20-39) top the list of users, followed by people aged 50 and above. More people from deprived areas use the services. Referrals take place mainly during office hours (including self-referrals) and the peak day is Wednesday. The life events which people indicate as related to their crisis have all to do with family dynamics and relationships, such as a row with one's partner or child (Rijnder, 1992).

A five year follow-up study in one area, which was carried out between 1985 and 1990 (Wundrik, 1992), highlighted the profile of the frequent user of the service. This tends to be one of a single young person, who has never been married, is less well educated than the majority of the population, is without close intimate relationships or a social network, and who is assessed as functioning socially at a low level. This frequent user is also likely to have had repeated admissions to psychiatric facilities, and to be diagnosed as suffering from schizophrenia, personality disorder or to have a dual diagnosis. Thirty-two per cent of the service users studied by Wundrik were judged as being a danger to themselves, and 20 per cent as presenting a risk to others. In terms of outcomes, up to 50 per cent of those referred to the service end up being admitted to hospital, 17 per cent of these admissions being involuntary.

The high level of referral for hospital admission may be the result of a number of factors, such as the severity of the crisis, the degree of risk to oneself or others exhibited, the lack of sufficiently supportive services in the community which could prevent admission (e.g. residential facilities, day care, counselling, training and work opportunities, mutual support), the very short period of crisis intervention (up to 72 hours), or the belief of the professionals in the usefulness of such admissions.

When assessed by Wolf (ibid.) in the 1980s over a period of several years, the initial crisis response model was found wanting in lacking specific objectives, follow-up planning, and poor assessment of skills and disabilities. Focusing on crisis services in Groningen (northern Holland) Wolf found that the services worked mainly with people known to the psychiatric system, whom she called 'old hands'. At the same time she indicates that the service provided a safety net for 14 per cent of its users who were experiencing their first mental breakdown and for whom it provided their first contact with the psychiatric system.

Wolf highlights the existence of poor multidisciplinary collaboration, though it is unclear whether this typifies the crisis service specifically or the whole psychiatric system. The quality of multidisciplinary relationships is traced by Wolf to the blurring of professional roles. The blurring is connected with each profession having inadequate knowledge of what the disciplines can do, leading to inadequate use of their expertise. She asserts that the existing services tend to overestimate users ability and readiness to take responsibility for their lives, and that there is a reluctance among professionals to intervene in people's lives, on the grounds of respecting citizens rights.

Wolf's evaluation led her to establish the pilot project of care management in the Netherlands, titled 'care innovation', which follows loosely the American assertive outreach model. The question remains whether the three cornerstones of her critique – namely the lack of good enough follow up and planning; poor multidisciplinary work and lack of professional expertise; and the assumed mistaken beliefs of the professionals – can be put at the door of crisis services specifically, or whether they are problems besetting the Dutch mental health system and in turn reflected also in the crisis services.

It would seem that Wolf herself and de Smit (1969, 1978) believe that crisis services were established as one of the strategies to solve the problems inherent in the mental health system in the first place. Wolf mentions the 'chronic crisis' of the services and de Smit writes about the politics of the services and their low credibility with the public.

A crisis service cannot fulfil its functions on its own. For example, it cannot avert admissions on its own, as it relies on other networks, facilities and services both to continue after the point at which it stops, following what usually amounts to a very short period of involvement with the user, as well as to precede its intervention. Thus even if the service offers a solid and intensive piece of work, the outcomes depend on what happens before and after people used this specific service. If people do come at an advanced stage of a mental illness crisis invariably they would need an asylum facility or people to stay with them around the clock for more than 72 hours. If people leave a crisis centre only to step back into the situation which contributed significantly to their crisis then the likelihood is that the crisis point will be soon reached again.

Wolf's wish for continuity of service cannot be realistically provided by a service based on 72 hours of intervention. A high level of burnout among workers in crisis services has been noted by some of the Dutch researchers (Kool and de Beers, 1992). This finding, not unique to the Netherlands, can be explained in a number of ways, including the frustration created by the very partial results that a service of such a short duration can achieve, the constant confrontation with a high level of suffering, confusion and risk. It is proposed that continuous peer support and extra free time may help to reduce the burnout level. I would add that this type of work would suit some professionals rather than others. Some workers enjoy the heightened atmosphere of a crisis service, the brief contact and relief offered, the assessment and brokerage functions. Others find it both difficult and unsatisfactory. Thus staff selection is an important issue here.

Noorlander (1992) is raising an interesting issue in proposing separate crisis services for those who abuse alcohol and those who abuse drugs. He argues that when alcoholics are placed together with people suffering from mental illness the tendency to deny the alcohol abuse is increased. Drug addicts need an environment in which the taken for granted rules of social and personal behaviour are repeatedly spelled out, as they have not internalised these rules at the time the addiction has began.

North American Experiences

A range of crisis services exists in the USA, developed from the late 1960s and early 1970s onwards, as one of the responses to the closure of psychiatric hospitals during that period. It is interesting to note that although community mental health centres developed from the late 1950s and were legislated as the centrepiece of mental health services in 1963, this has not led to the creation of crisis facilities. It would seem that crisis facilities have been established mainly to meet an asylum function. It is assumed here that the reader is familiar with the history and structure of mental health services in the USA, and hence only a very brief summary is provided.

The USA moved from a hospital-based system to a community-based system in the late 1960s and early 1970s in the wake of three main orientations (Brown, 1985):

- critique of the institutional nature of the hospitals regime;
- demonstrated success of rehabilitation programmes for clients receiving long term care in the community; and
- the wish of both central and state governments to cut down public expenditure.

The closure was often wholesale, administrative in nature, and with no attention to the processes of closure and its significance to patients, staff, and the general public. Apart from accommodation and income to survive with, little attention was paid to secure meaningful day activities for the resettled population. State psychiatric hospitals – similar to the British special hospitals – continued to exist, and specialised closed facilities came into being. These closed facilities may have up to one hundred people resident, with inmates staying for periods up to one year. They are owned and run by private corporations who are in the business to make profit. The profit is made by employing very few qualified professionals and a number of psychiatric technicians. In addition to the state psychiatric hospitals and the closed facilities, there are psychiatric wards in general hospitals with up to 25 beds each.

It took a long time for the mental health system (as distinct from model programmes) to accept the need for continuous work with the group of service users who have been resettled from the shut down hospitals. No overall strategy has been developed to meet the specific needs of the younger subgroup of them later termed 'the new long stay', or to secure the housing rights of the resettled ex-patients. When the areas they were housed in were bought by private companies and gentrified, the rent was too high for them to meet and many of them became homeless. Instead of making the connection between vulnerability and homelessness, a number of prominent psychiatrists proposed instead that because of their mental illness these people became homeless and led the life of petty criminals.

Many, though not all of the community mental health centres, tend to work predominantly with people suffering from milder mental health problems, as do the private for-profit therapeutic centres and office psychiatrists. The private not-for-profit sector provides accommodation, therapeutic communities for young people with long term mental illness, counselling, employment and advocacy services.

Case management was introduced in the USA in the early 1970s, and was implemented right across the board for all people with a serious and enduring disability. The aim was to try to overcome the fragmentation of the service system and the difficulties experienced in multidisciplinary work. Assertive outreach projects were established in some places, but are not available across the country (Test and Stein, 1985). An active user movement advanced advocacy initiatives and some separatist services which are run by users (Chamberlin, 1978).

It was only in the late 1970s that the gaps in the system were acknowledged and an attempt made by the National Institute of Mental Health to create a stakeholders strategy that would lead to a comprehensive and less fragmented system (Srole, 1991). This is a very difficult task to achieve in a country where there is no national health service and where one needs to show membership in an insurance scheme or eligibility for public service whenever a mental health intervention is called for. Many insurance schemes limit the period of psychiatric hospitalisation to no more than one month per year and out-patient psychiatry to no more than three months per year. Thus the focus on short interventions, including crisis work, is to a considerable extent motivated by financial reasons. The services range from telephone lines to a combined day hospital and residential crisis respite programme, through family placements, halfway houses and crisis hostels. Different types of evaluation have also been applied to these services, and will be looked at below.

Family placements for crisis care have been in operation far longer than any professional placement. Crisis homes in Denver (Polak and Kirby, 1976) and Minneapolis (Leaman, 1987) were the first to develop in the USA in the post-war period, though the first known such scheme began in 1880, based on similar European initiatives (Searight and Searight, 1988). They offer a number of advantages (Polak, Deveer and Kirby, 1977; Britton and Mattson-Melcher, 1985; Bennett, 1995):

- minimising stigma and fostering an ordinary living;
- providing a more individualised approach rarely possible in more crowded options;
- offering a nonprofessional home environment within which the person cared for is a guest rather than a patient;
- being possible to be set up in a variety of neighbourhoods; and
- avoiding the need to use the more expensive and alienating option of hospital admission (the cost of such a stay is around 30 per cent of the cost of a stay in an in-patient facility).

But they also have a number of disadvantages:

- not being open to self-referral;
- being likely not to be suitable for people at a high risk to themselves or to others;
- requiring carefully thought through matching of patients to families (e.g. in relation to ethnicity, age, and gender);
- relying on support being available to the carers around the clock. (At times this support has been found to be needed when a family placement resident has committed suicide after their stay); and
- involving liability issues which need to be acknowledged and dealt with.

Writing about the Crisis Home Programme of Dane County, Bennett (1995) points out that it is located within the Emergency Services Unit which includes a suicide prevention phone staff, social workers, support staff, nurses, psychologists and psychiatrists. For him the crisis homes have three major roles:

- as alternatives to in-patient stays (for about 40 per cent of the referrals);
- to facilitate early release from an in-patient facility (40 per cent);
- to prevent pre-crisis from escalation (20 per cent).

Families are recruited through an advertisement, then screened and trained. Trainers include experienced home providers and former clients; the emphasis being on the provision of a home environment, rather than on becoming mini-professionals. Relatively few families remain in the programme. Having children around is a positive predictor of retention (Rubin, 1990). Average length of stay has been three to five days. Difficult to place people – i.e. those with personality disorder – did not behave as such within the homes. Some of them use crisis homes on a regularly agreed basis, as a respite facility.

Both clients and the providers rate these schemes highly (Bennett, 1995; Leaman, 1987). The rate of hospital admission after a stay in such a home was 10-25 per cent, much lower than rates reported by other crisis facilities. Yet the use of this option is not widely diffused in the USA. Bennett suggests that this is due mainly to the reluctance of professionals to take it up and to over-reliance on professionals among the general public.

Cedar House in Boulder, Colorado, represents residential crisis facilities based in the community, run by professionals (Warner, 1992). The house is situated in a middle class area and has all of the amenities that such houses and neighbourhoods offer. People are referred in an acute mental illness crisis, often in a psychotic state. A neat bedroom, full board, assessment, medication, counselling and advice, group sessions, joint activities (e.g. cooking, shopping, playing music, singing) individualised outings (e.g. to one's home) are on offer. In return they have to abstain from the use of alcohol and drugs on the premises, help with the house chores, comply with prescribed medication, and see their key worker daily. The house is unlocked, and ordinary health facilities are used when in need. 'Many patients are treated involuntarily at Cedar House... they accept necessary restrictions because the alternative is hospital treatment which virtually none prefers' (ibid., pp. 116-117). It costs about a quarter of a hospital bed ($110 per day vs. $500 in 1991) (Warner, 1991, p. 116). The largely successful use of Cedar House has meant that the ten-bedded ward in the general hospital is usually under-occupied. People sent to hospital are those few who exhibit violence and are not ready to comply with Cedar House regulations. The Cedar House model too is to be found only infrequently elsewhere in the USA, perhaps because of fear generated by a severe mental health crisis.

The Department of Mental Health in New Haven, Connecticut, offers a programme aimed at handling crisis through a mixture of day hospital (Day Hospital of the Connecticut Mental Health Centre) care and care at a professionally staffed crisis house (Brownell House), with facilities at an in-patient unit also available. The mental health centre is operated by the Department of Psychiatry at Yale University, funded by the state. It aims 'to provide comprehensive mental health services for poor and severely mentally ill people' (Sledge et al., 1995, p. 236) within the catchment area. The degree of stigmatisation implied in putting together poverty with serious illness has escaped the creators of this scheme, as well as those who write about it.

The Day Hospital (DH) attempts to provide an alternative to acute in-patient admission and to act as a transition point for people discharged from in-patient facilities. It has 20 places, and about 220 people use it annually. Average length of stay is 30 days. Users are encouraged to use ordinary facilities and services while being in the day hospital, as well as to engage in voluntary work or a work placement.

Intervention by a multidisciplinary staff team includes individual work, family therapy and family work, and group therapy. A representative of the referring agency participates in the planning process, to ensure a seamless service when the person leaves the day hospital. Separate groups are run for people who have dual diagnosis. Other group activities focus on medication education, health promotion, sexual issues, life skills, and leisure time counselling. There is also a community meeting. An emergency telephone line is available to patients, and there is a 'back-up' bed on the in-patient unit. There are 12 full-time staff members (for 20 users).

The crisis house (CH) is managed by a private not-for-profit company, which provides other residential facilities for the mental health department. It is located in an apartment within a three-storey house in a middle class area, divided into three bedrooms, living room, dining room, office room, kitchen and bathroom. Those users who cannot continue with their ordinary activities are expected to participate in the day hospital. They are expected to assist with the house chores. Work with families takes place as needed. There are links to care management and out-patient facilities. The clinical responsibility is retained by the day hospital staff, in collaboration with the workers at Brownell House.

This programme has been evaluated by the use of randomised controlled trial methods. Excluded from the evaluation study were the following users:

- those on involuntary admission;
- those subject to physical restraints or demanding one-to-one attention;

- the acutely intoxicated;
- those suffering from a serious physical illness requiring hospital-based medical care; and
- those able to afford private services.

Only people judged as in need of psychiatric admission were invited to participate, thus excluding those suffering from acute mental distress but not in need of a hospital admission. One hundred and forty-six clients were recruited out of a total of 672 contacted, with 21 (14 per cent) subsequently dropping out. A number of symptom scales and social-psychological scales were administered: 11 in all. It is noteworthy that no one from the research team thought that this was asking too much of their respondents. Likewise, it seems that no one of the students of the project thought that they needed to talk to people using it and listen to their stories. Cost measures were also calculated. The results of this study can be summarised as follows:

- more men than women were found to have used the in-patient facilities and more women than men to have used the non in-patient services;
- the number of black people admitted to and referred to the service is much higher than is proportionate to their numbers in the catchment area population;
- 98 per cent of users were assessed as having an active psychiatric disorder, with 39 per cent diagnosed as psychotic, 52 per cent as suffering from a mood disorder, and 2 per cent from anxiety;
- 66 per cent were considered to be a risk to themselves;
- 22 per cent were considered to be a risk to others;
- 82 per cent had tried out-patient services unsuccessfully;
- there were no differences in symptom reduction between those attending in-patient and those in the DH/CH programmes;
- length of stay was shorter in the DH and CH than in the in-patient facility (17.2 days vs. 24.4 days);
- readmission rate was higher for the DH and CH than for the in-patient facility, though the difference did not reach statistical significance (43 per cent vs. 31 per cent);
- there was no difference in the social and psychological adjustment measures for the participants in the two programmes; and
- unit costs are considerably different. The in-patient unit costs $514 per day, the DH $157, CH $192. Even when calculated per episode, in which people might have moved between facilities, the DH and CH

combination costed between 63 per cent and 78 per cent of that of the mainly in-patient based intervention.

The researchers concluded that the DH and CH combination treats the same population as the in-patient unit, that its results are superior for 25 per cent of the group, and that it is 22 per cent more cost effective. Its main effectiveness lies in the treatment of the initial episode, and in this sense it does not simply delay hospitalisation but functions 'as a true alternative to hospitalisation' (Sledge et al., 1995, p. 49).

The attractiveness of the combined day hospital and crisis home lies in the provision of a comprehensive service and a clear medical focus, yet one which does not exclude psychological and social interventions. It also tends to be longer in duration than is the case for the family placements and for most of the people staying in Cedar House.

The question is whether this is necessary and is more effective than the two other options. The comparison has not been carried out up to now, and hence the following thoughts are speculative.

It is difficult to judge how many of the people using family placements would be assessed as in need of an in-patient facility from the outset. It is assumed here that the majority would not, but a minority would, as the people who use family placements have frequently utilised in-patient facilities in the past.

In contrast, all of the people in Cedar House would be seen as suitable for an in-patient admission if they lived in New Haven. As the outcomes from Cedar House are as good as those from the DH and CH in New Haven, it would seem that pertaining to effectiveness, there is no need for the very elaborated system created in New Haven. The need for the DH and CH combination seem to be more related to cultural fears and professional fears about people in a severe mental distress crisis.

Trieste, Italy

Trieste has epitomised the success of the Italian psychiatric reform since the 1970s. The reform, legislated in 1978, has focused on the participatory closure of psychiatric hospitals, relocation of a small number of beds in general hospitals, the creation of community mental health services around mental health centres, systematic work on the reintegration of the resettled patients and new users, and an attempt to change public attitudes (Mauri, 1986; Burti and Mosher, 1989; Ramon, 1990). Most of these features are to be found in the mental health services of Trieste; yet the Trieste model of these services is rarely copied elsewhere in Italy. We will come to this specific issue at the end of the description of the work of these services.

Italy legislated the introduction of a national health service in the same year in which the psychiatric reform law was passed (1978). These two reforms were part of a series implemented during the 1960s and 1970s, through which civil restrictions on abortion and divorce were lifted, and a large scale desegregation of children with disabilities was carried out in the educational system (Salvi and Checcini, 1990).

Trieste is located in the northeast of the country; the borders with Croatia and Slovenia lie within a short journey outside it. Indeed Trieste was strongly influenced, up to the end of the First World War, by its being a part of the Austro-Hungarian empire, whilst its more recent history reflects its location at the 'meeting point' between Italy and the former Yugoslavia. This cultural heritage can be seen in some of the buildings and coffee places, as well as in the literature produced by local authors.

Less widely known is the degree of strife in this bi-cultural city between Italians and Slovenians, between the Communists and the Fascists, between those who wish to remain part of Italy and the separatists. The latter are further divided into those who dream of an Isterian republic and those who would like to be part of Padania, the Veneto and Lombardia-based League. The aftermath of the Second World War was celebrated by a massacre of Fascists by Communists, in retaliation for the rather brutal killings of Communists by Fascists during the German occupation.

Trieste was ruled by Britain on behalf of the Allies between 1945 to 1954, as it proved difficult to reach a quick agreement as to whether it should be returned to Italy, be part of Yugoslavia, or become an autonomous city. It has 300,000 inhabitants. The city acts as the provincial centre for the region of Friuli Julia.

Trieste has the highest number of elderly people in Italy, most of them living on their own, thus not conforming to the myth of the extended, warm, Italian family. The suicide rate has been higher than in other places *prior* to the introduction of the psychiatric reform, perhaps due to the combination of old age and loneliness. There is no evidence to suggest that the suicide rate has become higher since the reform has been introduced. Italian psychoanalysis has a stronghold in the city, of which there is not even a whiff within the public sector mental health services. Psychoanalysis in Trieste is guarded by gurus from Slovenia within the private sector.

The current pattern of mental health services in the city was developed from the late 1960s onward, and is still evolving. Prior to 1968 the psychiatric hospital, with its one thousand beds, dominated the services. There were some out-patient clinics, but nothing else. The hospital was fairly traditional, in that all wards were closed, people stayed for a long time, were treated with medication and subject to a custodial regime, and that there were some workshops on the premises. The university clinic occupied one of the wards, and was selective as to who it would treat. Invariably the less serious cases found their way there.

Film and video clips demonstrate how institutionalised the hospital regime was, patients being without individualised clothing, being bathed with a hose pipe, and being taken for walks en-masse. Very few of the residents continued to be visited by their relatives. Most of the in-patients had no idea of how to use money, and had not visited any facilities in the city for as long as they could remember since entering the hospital.

Although initially the hospital was built outside town, with the later urban development which spread around it, especially in the 1950s, the hospital became part of a built neighbourhood, well within the city boundaries. Yet no one from the city came to visit the hospital, unless they came on business. Children, people with learning difficulties and people suffering from epilepsy, were also lumped together with the long-term in-patient population. The oral testimonies of the in-patients collected in the 1960s and the 1970s by the reform group highlight the sense of despair and isolation felt by them (Basaglia, 1968).

It is against this background that we need to assess the new services, and especially their crisis response pattern. The hospital was closed in a process which took ten years, with considerable effort being put into involving the local community, by:

- resettling patients into small group homes unstaffed at night;
- organising as many as 60 per cent of the users into work co-operatives; and
- creating community mental health centres.

The services are structured around seven community mental health teams, of which six have between six to eight beds each, access to an eight-bedded emergency ward in the general hospital, group homes, work co-operatives, workshops space, a flat used as a centre for younger people, and a women-only centre.

On the site of the old hospital the following can be found:

- some sheltered flats with day staff only;
- the local community mental health centre;
- two neurological wards;
- an enclosed flat for three severely mentally and physically disabled people inherited from the psychiatric hospital days;
- a drug addiction treatment centre;
- co-operatives focused on leather work, media production (video and animation films), a cafeteria, a beauty salon, agriculture (with a shop at the entrance to the site), and carpentry;
- art and craft workshops;
- a research institute;
- the headquarters of the mental health services in the city; and
- the faculty of law of Trieste university (which is renting the space from the health service).

There is no psychiatric hospital, and the eight-bedded unit in the general hospital is usually empty. There is no crisis service per se. Each community mental health centre is open from eight in the morning until eight at night and acts as a drop-in as well as a place to which people come for set appointments. Domiciliary services are offered as part of the normal service. There is an out-of-hours service during the night and the weekend manned by nurses and psychiatrists, and the emergency ward is also available for those who need it during the night.

In the morning each mental health centre phones to find out if people from the catchment area have been admitted to the emergency ward. If that turns out to be the case, the staff take them to the centre. In the centre a decision will be made as to whether they need to be resident, to use only the day centre or the night centre, to join specific activities, or be compulsorily admitted. Compulsory admission will mean, in this instance, the client staying put in the open centre. The centre will offer medical treatment, lunch either on the premises or in the nearby trattoria, tea/coffee on the premises, and participation in the various group activities which take place at the centre. These are run according to the level of demand. The centre may arrange a family meeting, and most centres now provide a relatives group. Rarely do the various groups of the centres focus on psychotherapeutic issues as such, though issues of loneliness, suffering, difficulties in relationships with significant others, and drug or alcohol abuse come up frequently in the informal discussion which takes place.

Most centres have no designated and separate staff room, though there is a medication cabinet in one of the rooms and that room would look like an office. A typical centre will have, in addition to the office room, two to three bedrooms, a large activities lounge, a quiet activities room, a dining and kitchen area, bathrooms, a piano, a television (often off), and table games.

Often centres have specific projects carried out in the community, for the community, and with other partners from the community. These would range from giving talks about mental illness at the local secondary school and inviting pupils to come to the centre, through mounting an exhibition of works of art by a user or a local resident at the centre, to participation in a demonstration or a neighbourhood festivity. A focus on cultural activities is maintained throughout, which could manifest itself in a poetry reading group, a theatre production, centre users going out together, or the centre's participation in local cultural events. Discussions between a user and his or her key worker may well be listened to by other users, who might also 'chip in', and are not discouraged from discussing the problems of others. At times, however, a user or a worker may suggest a meeting just for the two of them, in which case they will use one of the available rooms, or ask people to vacate a room for the duration of the meeting. Mutual support thus takes place informally.

There are daily staff meetings after lunch time, when the afternoon shift workers arrive. These act as 'handing over' meetings, as well as a space in which to discuss more general issues. Users can participate if they wish, including listening when matters related to other users are discussed. Thus confidentiality has a different meaning there from the one given in the British context. The Italians would argue that this format makes for a freer and more open exchange and involvement of users with staff than is possible within the British framework, as well as acting to inhibit some staff members from using careless or derogatory language. There are however individual patients files, and these are kept in a cupboard. Very little is written in them though, with most of the decisions, including those concerning medication, being written into a log book – another inheritance from the hospital regime. People can refer themselves to any part of the system, or can be referred by relatives, neighbours, other agencies.

The Trieste staff argue that there is no need for a special crisis service if community services are easily accessible, available, and trusted by the general public. Furthermore, they consider that a specialised service would give the wrong message, namely that only when your difficulties reach a crisis level will you be deserving special attention. The high level of informality of the service, and the availability of food and cultural activities, are perceived as important elements in creating an atmosphere in which the intensity of the suffering is reduced because the person feels included and welcomed as a person.

The evidence demonstrates that about 3,000 people use the Trieste mental health services annually. There have been only 64 people compulsorily admitted over the ten year period between 1978 to 1988 (Sain, Norcio, and Malannino, 1990). Thus the vast majority of patients have come into the community mental health centres under the terms of what would be called a voluntary admission in Britain. However, the number of people needing to stay overnight in the centres has declined to the point that two neighbouring centres decided in 1993 to amalgamate their bed facilities. Only one of them now offers such a facility, the merger having effectively cut down the number of beds available in the city by six out of the previous 50+. Instead of accommodation, the centre with no beds offers more group activities to which people from both localities can come. As the two localities are within a distance of five kilometres, and domiciliary visits are easily available, the added journey burden is insignificant.

The number of residents from Trieste to be found in the psychiatric prisons (similar to our special hospitals) during the 1978 to 1988 period was six. The psychiatrists work in liaison with these institutions and have taken out some of the inmates on conditional parole, a situation in which a specific community mental health centre becomes formally responsible for supervision and support in the community. There have been two homicides committed by known service users during these ten years, and one by a person on parole in the early 1990s. Inevitably these killings led to a heated public debate as to the responsibility of the psychiatric services in the tragedies. Two of the psychiatrists were brought to court and then absolved of guilt for their part in one of these homicides. One of the two psychiatrists has published a monograph detailing evidence given at the trial together with summaries of meetings with the woman user who killed her four year old son (Toresini, 1996). The monograph aims at making sense of what happened from the perspective of the woman as well as from that of the psychiatrists involved. It makes for very sad reading, while raising the issue of where the responsibility lies in the case of a client who was seen only twice and refused further contact at a point in time at which the homicidal thoughts were not known to the psychiatrists, but at which a deterioration in managing her life could have been predicted.

Experience has also indicated that as services became more known to the public, referrals come at an earlier stage in the cycle of mental distress crisis.

It has therefore become easier to arrest the further development of such a crisis and diffuse its stormy potential.

The general outcomes of the services in Trieste illustrate that it is possible for a community of this size to contain and offer services to people with mental illness, foster social integration, and encourage early referrals, all this without recourse to hospital beds and without a dedicated crisis service. To an extent the services in Trieste could be described as adhering to the model of home treatment, given the high number of home visits carried out there. However, home interventions happen in other Italian and non-Italian cities which have been less successful than Trieste in terms of the five outcomes outlined on page one. It would seem that what is unique in the Trieste model is the dedication to the provision of a neighbourhood service which provides psychiatric and social interventions on very flexible terms, side by side with continuing work on integration and involvement with the non-mentally ill community. An important distinguishing feature is the participation of people from the latter population in a variety of centre activities and efforts.

It was mentioned above that this model is not imitated elsewhere in Italy. It would be more accurate to say that it is not imitated in its entirety, while some of its elements are copied elsewhere. The component which is unique to Trieste and is left untouched by other places is that of the availability of beds in the mental health centres, the reliance on these beds within an open facility for compulsory admission, and the absence of a hospital ward. This is also the component which leads to disbelief among Anglo-Saxon visitors, readers or listeners to presentations about Trieste. It signifies the lack of fear of people with mental illness and the trust which the service providers extend to them. Perhaps this has been possible to establish and maintain in Trieste because of the dedication of the professionals working there, the high level of peer support, and the ability to generate a level of community and political backing which transcends party political boundaries. The success of the Trieste model is also attested to by the fact that there has not been any call to re-open the psychiatric hospital, or to legislate for programmes of supervised discharge. Nor has there been pressure for closed, intensively staffed, small residential facilities to be established, in order to care for the people that we in Britain are so afraid of, who are often dubbed as being challenging or 'difficult to place'.

Discussion and Conclusions

The descriptions of crisis services, and the findings of those who have evaluated them, which I have outlined above, raise a number of important issues, which can be itemised as follows.

a) Crisis intervention schemes are effective in providing alternative asylum facilities to about half of the people using them. The subgroups included here are:

- people with a first ever serious mental distress crisis (between 14–20 per cent of all users), for whom the services provide not only an asylum facility but also a way of not entering the career of a mentally ill patient;
- people with repeated episodes of hospital admission, who prefer not to go to the hospital. For this group crisis services enable the hospital and everything that it symbolises to be avoided. In addition, an opportunity to search for other interventions and solutions to those of hospital treatment, within in a safe and more hopeful environment is provided (45 per cent); and
- people who come into the schemes because of alcohol and drug abuse problems, which at the time of entry take the form of mental illness. It is doubtful as to whether a mental health crisis service offers this group what it needs, even if at the time of the crisis it meets the urgent need for asylum and assessment.

b) The fact that half of the referrals end up in a hospital admission where hospitals exist as the main in-patient facility may mean that:

- the in-patient facility is using the crisis scheme for screening purposes;
- the assessment system in place is either insufficiently sensitive, or too influenced by financial considerations; and
- crisis intervention schemes do not offer safe enough options.

c) The findings that residential crisis houses and mental health centres with beds offer an effective and viable alternative to both in-patient and short term, largely nonresidential crisis facilities in both Boulder and Trieste highlight the fact that the core issue relates to ideologies and beliefs about serious mental illness, and not to the effectiveness of community-based, open facilities. The effectiveness of the services in Boulder and Trieste covers all of the subgroups of users mentioned above, and meets the need for asylum with dignity, safety, accessibility, availability, and responsiveness, as well as satisfying the financial criteria of funders.

d) The differences between the Boulder system and that in Trieste need to be looked at carefully. It would seem that Trieste has managed to provide a good quality crisis intervention service without a dedicated space for it, apart from the emergency ward in the general hospital. The need to have a separate house in Boulder together with a psychiatric ward in the general hospital is perhaps a reflection of a system in transition, where the providers – and maybe the local population too – are as yet unsure if a new and pioneering system can cope with the risk inherent in crisis work.

e) Family placements offer a good alternative for a number of people in a crisis, but are unlikely to provide it for the majority of people in a mental health crisis. Therefore this option should be available, but not on its own.

f) Crisis services can operate usefully only within a good enough mental health system; they cannot fully achieve their objectives on their own.

Looking at the implications of the different options for Britain, it is necessary to take account of where we are now. It seems to me that we are currently:

- preoccupied with safety issues and faced with a media keen to demonise people with serious mental health problems and lay the blame when things go wrong at the door of professional services;
- opting for very costly secure unit schemes. These are costly not only in financial terms, but also in reintroducing social segregation and in giving succour to the fears of the public;
- working within a narrow legislative focus on supervision registers and supervision discharge orders;
- lacking in and overall strategy for the new long stay and especially for the younger group within this category;

- at the stage of trying out different home treatment schemes;
- beginning to experiment with outreach services;
- in the position of having very few residential crisis facilities;
- not having diffused knowledge about successful crisis intervention experiences (such as the Barnet intensive crisis intervention) despite the clear evidence as to their effectiveness;
- struggling with a mental health system that is far from being either seamless or comprehensive. In particular it omits vocational training and employment as viable options for people over 30, with professional workers not being trained to even look at this important area of people's lives; and
- stuck with a focus on people with serious mental illness which, though it has been overdue because of the lack of such a focus in the past, has led to a situation now where there is neglect of the needs of people with milder mental health problems beyond medication. This neglect undermines the objective of secondary prevention and increases the demand for crisis services.

Taking into account this rather long list, it would seem that we need to experiment with a range of crisis intervention options and carefully evaluate them. Services which already have well developed home treatment systems and which do not simply copy the medical model, could experiment with either the Boulder or the Trieste options.

However, unless we work on achieving a shift in the beliefs system pertaining to people suffering from mental illness of the media, the politicians, the general public and mental health professionals, we will continue not to have viable responses to crisis.

References

Basaglia, F. (ed.) (1968), *L'istituzione negata*, Einuadi, Milan.
Bennett, R. (1995), 'Family Placement Schemes as an alternative to short-term hospitalisation', in Phelan, P., Strathdee, G. and Thornicroft, G. (ed.), *Emergency Mental Health Services in the Community*, Cambridge University Press, Cambridge.
Britton, J.G. and Mattson-Melcher, D.M. (1985), 'The crisis home: sheltering patients in emotional crisis', *Journal of Psychosocial Nursing and Mental Health Services*, Vol. 23, pp. 18–23.
Brown, P. (1985), *The Transfer of Care*, Routledge, London.
Burti, L. and Mosher, L. (ed.) (1989), *Community Mental Health: Principles and Practice*, Norton, New York.

Chamberlin, J. (1978), *On Our Own*, McGraw Hill, New York.

de Smit, R. (1969), *Function and policy of the crisis centre in community psychiatry*, Paper given at the 125th annual meeting of the American Psychiatric Association, Miami, May 5th.

de Smit, R. (1978), *Crisis Intervention and Systems Change: Pitfalls of social planning*, Paper given at the VIIth World Congress of Social Psychiatry, Lisbon, 8–14 October.

Kool, J. and de Beers, M. (1992), 'Is prevention of psychiatric admission feasible?', in van Luyn, J. (ed.), *Emergency Psychiatry Today*, Elsevier, the Hague.

Leaman, K. (1987), 'A hospital alternative for patients in crisis', *Hospital and Community Psychiatry*, Vol. 38, pp. 1221–3.

Mauri, D. (ed.) (1986), *La liberta e terapeutica?*, Feltrinelli, Rome.

Noorlander, E.A. (1992), 'Specialised crisis intervention units for drug and alcohol addicts: are they necessary?', in van Luyn, J.B. (ed.), *Emergency Psychiatry Today*, Elsevier, the Hague.

Polak, P., Deever, S. and Kirby, M. (1977), 'On treating the insane in sane places', *Journal of Community Psychiatry*, Vol. 5, pp. 380–7.

Polak, P. and Kirby, M. (1976), 'A model to replace psychiatric hospitals', *Journal of Nervous and Mental Disease*, Vol. 163, pp. 13–22.

Querido, A. (1969), 'The Shaping of Community Mental Health Care', *British Journal of Psychiatry*, Vol. 114, pp. 293–302.

Ramon, S. (ed.) (1990), *Psychiatry in Transition: British and Italian Experiences*, Pluto Press, London.

Rijnder, C.A. (1992), 'Who are the clients of crisis centres?', in van Luyn, J.B. (ed.), *Emergency Psychiatry Today*, Elsevier, the Hague.

Rubin, J.S. (1990), 'Adult foster care for people with chronic mental illness', *Adult Residential Care Journal*, Vol. 4, pp. 5–19.

Sain, F., Norcio, B. and Malannino, S. (1990), 'Compulsory health treatment: the experience of Trieste from 1978 to 1988', *For Mental Health*, Vol. 4, pp. 137–52.

Salvi, E. and Checcini, M. (1990), 'Children with handicaps in ordinary schools', in Ramon, S. (ed.), *Psychiatry in Transition*, Pluto Press, London.

Searight, H.R. and Searight, P.R. (1988), 'The homeless mentally ill: overview, policy implications and adult foster care as a neglected resource', *Adult Foster Care Journal*, Vol. 2, pp. 235–57.

Sledge, W.H., Tebes, J. and Rakfleldt, J. (1995), 'Acute Crisis Respite Care', in Phelan, P., Strathdee, G. and Thornicroft, G. (eds), *Emergency Mental Health Services in the Community*, Cambridge University Press, Cambridge.

Srole, B. (1991), *Profiles of Psychiatric Crisis Response Systems*, National Institute of Mental Health, Rockville, Maryland.

Test, M.A. and Stein, L. (eds) (1985), 'The training in Community Living Model: A decade of Experience', *New Directions for Mental Health Services*, Vol. 26, Jossey-Bass, San Francisco.

Toresini, L. (1996), *La Testa Talgiata*, Gutenberg, Trieste.

Warner, R. (1991), 'Building Programmes', in Ramon, S. (ed.), *Beyond Community Care: Normalisation and Integration Work*, Mind/Macmillan, London.

Wolf, J. (1992), 'Psychiatry old hands: about dilemmas in psychiatric care', in van Luyn, J. (ed.), *Emergency Psychiatry Today*, Elsevier, the Hague.

Wundrik, A. (1992), 'The revolving door client of crisis intervention services', in van Luyn, J. (ed.), *Emergency Psychiatry Today*, Elsevier, the Hague.

11 Progress and Prospects for Crisis Services

DYLAN TOMLINSON

Introduction: The Policy Background

Crisis services have received little consideration in the development of UK mental health policy. This is because such services neither offer scope for the rehabilitation and resettlement of long stay hospital patients nor for elaboration of general hospital psychiatric functions. The closure of psychiatric hospitals, together with the 'reprovision' of their services in community settings, was arguably the dominant objective of government policy for much of the 1960s, 1970s and 1980s. The government demonstration of this policy, the closure of Powick hospital, in Worcestershire, evolved over the period between 1968 and 1988. At the same time, public awareness of conditions, staffing and treatment regimes within both mental illness and mental handicap hospitals was heightened by a succession of enquiries into their administration. The problems were not only to be addressed by improving management, but by breaking down institutions into to smaller scale neighbourhood units, where patients would have opportunities to participate in civic life and thereby, it was hoped, be less prone to neglect and abuse. Much policy making effort over this period was put into promoting the joint planning of community mental health services between district health authorities and local government social services departments. Progress in achieving this objective was inevitably slow. Indeed, Barbara Castle, who was Health Minister in 1975, pointed out that there was at that time 'little or no scope for substantial additional expenditure on health and personal social services'. This meant that the mental health service which would ideally be provided in all districts would be unlikely to be developed 'even within a twenty five year planning horizon' (DHSS, 1975, p. iii).

Better Services for the Mentally Ill (DHSS, 1975) can be seen, in retrospect, as an authoritative blueprint for local mental health services. The District General Hospital (DGH) service was at the centre, with normative requirements for the proportion of beds which might be provided for specified sizes of hospital catchment populations. Norms guidance for day hospital and day centre places were given on the same basis. The government acknowledged at the same time that local authority hostels, day centres and group homes, were required to enable the hospital service to be able to function adequately. But whereas the NHS was provided with the capital and revenue to develop DGH services by central government, there was no such funding to be made available to local government.

Joint Finance was set up in recognition of this deficit, but consisted merely of time limited grants from the NHS to local government, to support specified projects, generally over a three year period. At the end of this period the local government would have to take over responsibility for funding the said project itself.

It was for this reason that the (DHSS) Care in the Community paper of 1981 suggested that the NHS might need to fund local government projects in perpetuity, if the closure of psychiatric hospitals was to be achieved. Funding would be transferred from the budget of the closing hospital to the 'receiving' district health authority – to which patients for a particular project were to be resettled – with that authority then paying the local government agency providing the service to the resettled patients.

The closures thus provided both the main policy impetus and the funding impetus for the implementation of the Better Services blueprint, which, without wide variation has become the normative framework of UK mental health services.

Interestingly, the term crisis service was used only once in the Better Services document, to refer to the activity of a specialist multidisciplinary team, and especially to the role of community psychiatric nurses within it, linked to the DGH, if not to be based there, and able to respond to emergencies on a 24 hours a day basis. Crisis services were not seen to be a distinct 'alternative' in their own right, but rather as a form of hospital outreach integrated with primary care. The multidisciplinary team was envisaged as having district wide duties spanning hospital and community services, and the idea of district sectorisation for such teams, each sector team being under a Consultant lead, was floated. Thus the concept of the crisis service as an alternative to hospital, for a whole catchment population, was not apparent.

Crisis Services and Innovation

If one takes a historical view of the treatment meted out to those deemed mad, it has always revolved around prisons, the police or judiciary, and hospitals or infirmaries. The mad have been removed to corrective or curative institutions. There have of course been a number of innovators who, in various periods, attempted to develop humane forms of community, or domiciliary support and care. But one usually finds some form of heroic behaviour, or extraordinary, saintly tolerance at the heart of such efforts, which is therefore extremely vulnerable to project fatigue as the capacities of the innovator and followers are inevitably sapped by the demands of the task, and perhaps as much by their detractors, jealous of their popularity with those suffering from mental illness. The innovator also suffers from the invariably insecure basis on which the financing of their service depends, with the cossetting of philanthropist supporters a further source of energy deflection and depletion.

In the contemporary context, it is all too clear that crisis services do not fall within the trinity of prisons, police and infirmaries. As Scull (1996) points out, it is difficult to see how far humane mental health treatment can be funded unless it is medicalised. Crisis services are primarily non-medical means of intervention. Innovators are therefore bound to look to charities and to Social Service Departments. And indeed it appears to be the case today that without the support of charities such as the Mental Health Foundation, few innovators would be able to envisage a prospect of their approach being funded.

As far as Social Service Departments are concerned, the lack of priority for mental health after-care has been well documented, with the Joint Finance programme mentioned above having been followed by the Mental Illness Specific Grant, a similar attempt by central government to give a fillip to local initiatives. It is difficult to see local authorities, considered as a group, giving priority to mental distress in the foreseeable future, with growth in the numbers of elderly people as a proportion of the population to respond to, on the one hand, and their overriding social and statutory duty to protect children from neglect and abuse to be fulfilled on the other.

Recent policy initiatives in mental health have been designed to address what are considered to be problematic aspects of the hospital closures programme, responding to public and political anxiety about the perceived loss of the security function of the psychiatric hospital. The Care Programme Approach, Care Management, and the Mental Health (Patients in the Community) Act have all been concerned with arrangements for the continuing supervision of patients who have been discharged from psychiatric hospital treatment. It can be readily noted that this policy context of reinforcement for the hospital to the point of extending its authority into homes and neighbourhoods, is not one in which alternatives to the hospital admission and treatment process will enjoy credibility and political support. Moreover, the morale of social workers, the profession which is arguably the most associated with alternatives to hospital, has taken a considerable beating, with the attribution to them of repeated failures in high profile child protection cases, and they appear not to enjoy the confidence of the public.

Why Crisis Services?

Taking into account this context it is important to be able answer the questions of: (a) why crisis services might be preferable to conventional hospital services; and (b) why crisis services might be considered an advance in provision.

I will turn to these questions below, but before doing so I think it important to point out the awe inspiring breadth of concerns which crisis services, by their nature attempt to address. This breadth of concerns is opened up by the idea of intervening at the person's home where possible. In this respect their proponents and managers are immediately faced with a range of social problems which teams who admit patients in crisis to hospital do not face. Most obviously, assessing and supporting the individual's crisis at home, means addressing the home environment, always assuming of course, that the person has a home in which assistance can be given. The broader context of housing policy is a major factor in this regard. The large scale and enforced sale of Council houses and flats by local authorities during the last 20 years has had the inevitable consequence of significantly diminishing the availability of affordable housing, especially for single people. At the same time, the criteria for allocating the Council housing that remains has come to exclude all but the poorest, most needy and vulnerable households, a process referred to as social polarisation in which Council property is increasingly stigmatised and identified as undesirable ghetto accommodation (Forrest and Murie, 1991). This property moreover is the least desirable of the stock of 20 years ago in terms of fabric, location, repair. It is within some of these depressing settings, which one might justifiably refer to as chronically ill housing, that the attractively named home treatment of the crisis service comes to be given.

Almost as important an issue for crisis services is the social isolation which they confront in the domiciliary context. This isolation is an inevitable corollary of the fact that, in modern times, most people's extended family support networks are spread far and wide. Whilst the high contemporary rate of separation and divorce is not, as such, the issue here (marriage rates are also high, and it is, in mental health terms, difficult to choose between the merits of the conflict riven, walled-in-family, and the liberated, estranged family), the increasing proportion of households which are occupied by a single person has obvious consequences for home treatment regimes. The sufferer's family may be perhaps hundreds of miles distant, and partners, where they exist, may find it impossible to live with the crisis. In these situations, the ability of the treatment providers to nurture the coping capacity of the individual receiving support, in such a way as to give hope for continuity after the completion of the intervention, will be much impeded.

All of this has to be seen in the context of the perpetual struggle in the mental health context against institutionalisation and service dependency. That the nature of this struggle is often of an intense nature becomes clear where the conditions in which the person receiving the crisis service is living give little incentive for the person to 'make a go' of things on his or her own.

To What Extent are Crisis Services Preferable to Conventional Hospital Services?

Probably the most forceful argument in favour of crisis services, and perhaps, in our current historical period, the most legitimate, is that of service users who demand non-medical alternatives to hospital treatment. Here too, though, the arguments, in my view should be treated with some caution. Firstly, because the views of those service users who recover from their breakdowns after hospital treatment, and do not require service support thereafter, are not very often analysed. Secondly, because few would argue that consumerism is always a good in its own right. There is a certain 'sweet shop' analogy with health and welfare provision during the contemporary period by which providers are under pressure to make available those services which are most liked by users. But those most liked may not be the most beneficial in the long term, either from the users or the providers point of view. Equally, a less confrontative approach to a person in crisis, deemed supportive for that reason, may postpone attempts to resolve key issues for that person until entrenched defeatism and dependency has set in. In any case, if one looks at what is most valued by users, someone to talk to and confide in, and explanation about treatment and drugs available, such support can be provided by a range of different services, and is clearly not something that only crisis services, or non-hospital based services, can deliver.

Despite the formidable nature of the social problems which the non-medical home based alternatives are pitted against, the possibility of a noninstitutional response, in which the power of the medical regime is displaced is another strong argument in favour of crisis services. However it should be noted that not all crisis services are based on home treatment, and indeed the women-only service, one which has been the subject of some acclaim, at Drayton Park, in North London, provides a crisis house, at which sufferers are supported through their crises. One of the first 'home treatment' services, based in West Birmingham, which is medically led, but not institutional, still found it necessary to eventually set up a small respite house for its clients, in recognition of the importance of a break for the client from intractable home environment problems (see chapter 6 in this volume).

So it is still not clear that crisis services, as an alternative to hospital, are necessarily preferable as the means to address the problems which the sufferer has. As Hogan and Orme's chapter in this volume shows, whilst crisis services may be more popular, and may keep people out of hospital, the extent to which they improve the health of the sufferer and their carers over the medium and longer term is not always demonstrated. I have already commented on the heroic and admirable nature of the efforts of staff offering these services, as Radway's work in Birmingham, which she discusses in chapter 6, indicates.

Why are Crisis Services an Advance?

As Ramon suggests in her discussion of Dutch crisis services in the previous chapter, it is loading too much on to crisis services to ask that they can constitute an advance over conventional methods of responding to acute mental distress on their own. There are two senses, in this respect, in which it is difficult to regard crisis services as offering an advance. The first relates to their short term nature. The emphasis is on the individual being given intensive support to quickly find ways of coping with the factors which have led to crisis. This invites the accusation that such services are designed to push responsibilities – for housing, relationships, work – back on to those who are saying that they cannot deal with such responsibilities. Are they thus experienced as more oppressive than reception into hospital?

The second sense in which it is difficult to see how an advance might be constituted is in relation to the contemporary policy context with which they have to deal. The fact that they usually lack the facility for continuous surveillance during the period of response, assessment and intervention, militates strongly against non-medical and noninstitutional services being purchased by health and social services as a wholesale alternative to hospital psychiatry. The basis of the 1983 Mental Health Act is for the statutory authorities to intervene by removing those who are a serious danger to themselves or others to a safe place. Without that safe place being within their compass, it is difficult to see how crisis services, especially in inner cities, can offer the insurance against risk (problematic as it may well be in its current implementation in hospitals) that is a fundamental organising principle for medical and institutional responses. A corollary of the latter two points is that few crisis services are able to make their support available on an open access basis, and that many restrict their work to clients with known psychiatric histories: that is to say clients who have experienced their breakdown, or initial florid crisis, before the particular episode that the crisis service responds to. Generally these first crises will have been referred to hospitals.

The Concept of Crisis

The concept of crisis in itself represents a challenge to the psychiatric treatment milieu, and this can be seen to be part of its attraction to those who seek to break with the tradition of society representing and responding to bizarre or strange behaviour and beliefs as an illness. As Pilgrim notes in chapter 3, both the word mental and the word illness are highly problematic as terms which can be used with any degree of accuracy to convey the nature of the personal problems that the sufferer of crisis endures.

In some sense the adoption of the term crisis remains rather puzzling though, since it can certainly be seen to have some medical resonance outside the mental health context. Sufferers from the sickle cell disorder, for instance, are said to go into crisis, when the cell organisation in their body changes, causing them acute pain and physiological impairment. Nonetheless, in mental health terms, the word crisis can be seen to be one which 'normalises' mental illness. At the trivial extreme, people speak of being in a crisis when their washing machine has broken down, or when their pet cat has disappeared, or when they have lost their address book and are unable to make contact with work colleagues or friends. More serious disruptions of taken for granted social and personal props, such as where a person peremptorily loses his or her job or where a person is suddenly deserted by a partner of long standing, are also, to be sure, commonly conceptualised as personal crises. Crisis management, moreover, has the hallmarks of taking decisive action to prevent businesses or administrative entities from collapse. When these uses of the term are carried over into popular understandings of crisis intervention in mental health, its potency and cathartic potential can be anticipated.

The use of the concept of crisis is of great significance in distinguishing crisis services from community mental health teams or primary care services. This is because of the hypothesis about the nature of the critical personal problems which are involved in what would be conventionally termed a nervous breakdown or psychiatric emergency. What is understood by the term crisis by those who prefer to use it in describing the period of acute mental distress which is involved, is a failure of the ordinary coping and defence mechanisms with which the individual affected is ordinarily able to address the major problems that come his or her way in life. As Leiba points out in chapter 2, this is considered to be a temporary loss of such abilities, which will only obtain until the individual evolves new ways of handling the problems which beset him or her. The sufferer will be assisted in this process of adaptation and learning by the crisis service.

It will be quite clear to the reader that such a process does not, so far as it follows this course, involve any requirement for the individual affected to be 'under the doctor', or to be detained for their own or others safety. For many psychiatrists, such a view of the person in acute distress is quite misguided, since it is only addresses the superficial symptoms of what is, for them, the underlying illness. Crisis management can only address, for these critics, the way in which the illness manifests itself in eccentric behaviour and the sufferers often bizarre attempts to articulate their crisis situation and respond to it. The idea of crisis neglects the process of disease onset and the aetiology of an illness, which can be little understood without diagnosis and prognosis. Moreover, the idea of developmental and life crises does not provide an explanation of why it is that some people go into crises during the particular developmental stages which present them with special problems, or after particular life crises that are socially critical, while the vast majority of people do not.

The popularity of the crisis concept with users of mental health services (Wallcraft, 1996) possibly indicates that it has been imbued with therapeutic properties on account the fact that it has not been associated with abuse, detention without consent, and enforced treatment. Crisis perhaps also encapsulates a more optimistic view of ways in which the personal problems faced by those in acute distress can be resolved than other terms.

Garelick's (1988) observations on the roles played by enthusiasts for and detractors from psychiatric hospital closure, whilst somewhat over embellished, provide some illuminating insights into recent UK processes of mental health services development. Garelick argued that there was a manic element in the visionary work of those planning the replacement of mental hospitals, in that the process of 'reproviding' its facilities in the community was often believed to be of a very significant and intrinsic therapeutic value, such that future community services would be unlikely to have to treat so many apparently hopeless chronic cases as had been resident in the psychiatric hospitals. Those role players who pointed to the over optimism of this view were perhaps somewhat depressed in contrast to the more manic enthusiasts, since their life's work and vocation was implicitly being rejected.

As Matthews indicates in chapter 5, what the development of crisis services entails, taken to its more elaborate and extensive form, is a similar process of replacement of the district general hospital acute psychiatric wards. It is therefore probably highly likely that some of the issues analysed by Garelick will be identifiable if and when such a process gets under way.

An important factor in the earlier process of psychiatric hospital 'reprovision', and one which presented one of the most difficult problems to resolve, was the nature of involvement and inclusion of the staff within the hospitals which were being closed. Given their intimate roles in the discredited institutional warehousing and custodial regimes, how were these long term staff members to be pressed into community support teams and resource centres, requiring new brands of mental health teaching and learning to be operationalised (Ramon, 1992)? It is this question which also faces those who are developing crisis services, in so far as they seek to offer the same 'place of safety' or seek access to such a place of safety, and offer a quick domiciliary response to those who are extremely disturbed. They will inevitably require the co-operation and support of staff running the district general hospital psychiatric wards during the development process. They will also be seeking to recruit staff with experience of working in such a setting, since those settings are the places where one becomes skilled at communicating with, supporting, and supervising someone who is acutely distressed. This leads one to the conclusion that crisis services will usually have to seek to identify opinion leaders within the district general hospital who are prepared to participate in, and sanction, the deployment of DGH staff resources to the development of local alternatives to hospital.

Crisis Services and Community Support

If, as Ratna (1998) contends, crisis services are the bastard child of psychiatry, they perhaps reflect an earlier ideological phase in the history of health and welfare, when therapy through democratic community was an important principle. Crisis services, as Godin and Scanlon discuss in chapter 8, were first established during a period of therapeutic optimism in relation to mental health. Tooth and Brooke (1961) had published their prediction of a significant decline in the institutionalised population, through a combination of naturally occurring deaths due to old age, and planned discharges as a result of rehabilitation. Store-front, open access, community mental health centres were being developed on a large scale, through a federal initiative in the United States. This was a time when there were also high hopes of family therapy, the family having been identified since the time in which Freudian and Jungian analysis had been propounded, as a likely source of many of the anxieties and vulnerabilities of people suffering mental illness. It seemed to follow that the provision of support for families, giving them insight into how their interaction was related to the problems of the sufferer in their midst, could enable that person to begin to cope in their 'natural' setting. Policy makers and practitioners were optimistic that intensive community support services could sustain most people with mental health problems without recourse to hospitals.

The 'discovery' of some of the disadvantages of the community support system, such as the transinstitutionalisation described by Brown (1985) – the process of people being discharged from hospital into board-with-care homes or nursing homes, was still some way off. New professions were being set up as part of this process of community treatment of the mentally ill, in particular the community psychiatric nursing profession, which expanded its numbers dramatically in the 1960s and 1970s. An interesting feature of this development was that services were dependent on the new professions maintaining credibility and control within the framework of NHS care. Psychiatric Nurses had traditionally been doctors' assistants within hospital psychiatry. As they became established in semi-autonomous community teams, and later attached as quasi consultants to GP surgeries, they found welcome opportunities to liberate themselves from the control of the hospital psychiatrists. The profession of CPN became very attractive during this period of therapeutic optimism. The CPNs were also able to augment their skills by undertaking training in counselling and various forms of behaviour therapy. Social Workers were in a slightly different position, but also advancing as a group relative to the medical profession. The Seebohm Report of 1968 was designed to put their work on a surer professional footing, and it created the generic social worker who undertook specialist training in psychiatric social work after completing basic social work training.

A period of experimentation similar in some respects to the period in which Tuke and Pinel initiated their moral treatment at the end of the eighteenth century, could be identified in some daring and risky 1960s projects. Kingsley Hall in London's East End, with which R.D. Laing was associated, was perhaps the best known. A minimum of restrictions on behaviour was the aim, with residents being free to give vent to their feelings in a supportive setting. The experiment attracted students and intellectuals to work within it. Such ventures were to be found in the form of other residential therapeutic communities with similar objectives, and having minimal medical involvement. Few survived the therapeutic optimism which gave rise to them (Ingleby, 1990; Baruch, 1984).

The idea of crisis services was one which was also borne on the relatively unimpeded tide of public welfare expansion of the late 1950s to the mid 1970s. This was the period of the so-called consensus about government being charged with the responsibility for securing the health and welfare of its citizens. Its end was signalled by such writers as Robert Bacon and Walter Eltis, who in their series of 1975 *Sunday Times* articles (published during November of that year), attacked the state domination of health and social services as a factor which had greatly weakened Britain's economic performance. It was some time before the NHS was seriously affected by the changing political climate though. It had come out very creditably from an enquiry conducted early on in its history (Ministry of Health, 1956) into whether the increasing levels of spending on it was justified by the services provided. NHS growth in real terms was to continue even after the fiscal crisis of 1973, so that even the Thames Regions, which were over-resourced relative to the Northern and Midlands Regions of the NHS, continued to enjoy growth until the early 1980s. Hunter (1980) described the situation during these years as one of guided incrementalism. Whilst it obtained, crisis services had a reasonable chance of being guided into the then still increasing array the NHS functions.

When thinking about the evolution of the crisis concept and of early crisis services, it is also important to recall the significance of feminism, and of the Equal Pay Act and Sex Discrimination Acts which followed. If one looks back to such widely read contemporary works such as Ann Oakley's (1974) *Housewife*, which iterated the drudgery and oppression of the wife as domestic servant, it is easy to see how the popularity of such accounts, and their manifesto for social change, might induce a heady air of optimism about how the depressed women described in Brown and Harris' (1978) studies could be supported in a cathartic way by crisis and other community services.

Community is a term which many sociologists, as well as, so it would appear (Acheson, 1985) many medical practitioners, feel no longer has any descriptive value or explanatory power. Whilst it is associated with neighbourhood belonging, self help, and social networks in the context of community care, the difficulties of defining a community have proved to be legion. Nonetheless, the philosophy of community support lay behind much welfare policy in the 1960s and 1970s. It was particularly evident in the community development projects of the latter decade and in such academic works as that of Robinson and Abrams 1977 monograph, *What we know about the neighbours*, in which the relationship between the state and neighbouring was examined. With the coming of the welfare state, which can be regarded as a national community effort to address financial hardship, illness, unemployment and other social ills, inevitably the role of local helping networks diminished. Once the decline of community thesis became something which governments felt they needed to address, then it naturally affected the way in which crisis services were regarded. The key point was that those involved in planning health and social care recognised that community support networks could not be taken for granted, and that state resources, or financial assistance, would be necessary for local helping to be effected.

This context has been of critical importance for crisis services, as their successful operation inevitably rests, to a fair degree, on the availability of community resources and services to their clients, the premise being that use of facilities and amenities is integral to one's personal well being. With the restrictions imposed by successive governments on public services through the 1980s and into the 1990s (Bebbington and Kelly, 1995), the kind of facilities which people in crisis might avail themselves of, such as legal and money advice centres, social and drop-in centres, customised adult education classes, skills and training centres, health centres for the homeless and rootless, and so on, have clearly become difficult to identify. The possibilities for supporting people in crisis at home are inevitably affected by the contexts of restriction on services around them. Hospitals then remain the all encompassing, often demeaning, but sometimes only viable option.

Just as the profile of community support has declined, so that of risk management has come to increasing prominence, as has been noted by several contributors to this book. So much is this now so in mental health that the influential Sainsbury Centre decided to devote its annual Conference to the topic of risk evaluation and management during 1998. In this respect, crisis services rely heavily on their initial assessment of the situation in which the client is situated, since they rarely have access to 24 hours a day supervision facilities where risk can be assessed over several days. It seems to me that this is such a significant issue in the contemporary political climate that it very much argues in favour of closer collaboration between crisis services and hospital psychiatry.

Crisis Services and Key Contemporary Objectives for Mental Health Services

It is possible to get some idea of how far the development of crisis services may be able to move beyond the heroic local enthusiasts stage by considering the extent to which such services meet the key contemporary objectives for mental health services, which I suggest are as shown in Table 11.1 below, with risk and close supervision the most prominent to be borne in mind. By also examining the way in which the wider contemporary policy framework both supports and detracts from the progress of crisis services, as in Table 11.2 below, one can start to identify significant policy factors to take into account when considering the issue of elaborating crisis response in mental health further.

Table 11.1   Which typical UK mental health service objectives do crisis services satisfy?

Security	?
Safety	?
High staff/client ratio	+
Intensive support	+
Carers' involvement	+

Table 11.2   The policy environment for crisis services development

What policy factors work in favour of crisis?	What policy factors work against services development?
• Care for carers	• Emphasis on risk assessment scope for hospital staff development and management
• Community care policy	• Protection of community
• Support for users movement	• Criminal justice
• Joint health/social services	• Psychiatrists fighting for hospital commissioning services
• Least restrictive environment	• Lack of policy for alternatives to reception and hospital for reception purposes
• Treatment	• Approved Social Workers an under-resourced and constrained faction

Conclusion

Pilgrim's chapter suggests to me that a more legitimate description of the functions of acute mental health services would be one in which what might be termed a community support function be acknowledged as well as a crisis support function. Indeed, MIND's (1983) manifesto for mental health services, referred to crisis intervention *or* community intervention as an element of a comprehensive service, perhaps indicating the nature of conflict over whose interests are being pursued by an emergency service. A significant proportion of patients admitted, the majority in a number of areas, are being brought into hospital against their will. As Pilgrim notes, they are obviously not receiving the support which they would wish, at the time of admission. Whatever one believes about the rectitude of such a process, it cannot be denied that forcible detention is hardly likely to enable the person received into hospital to find their own ways of coping with a crisis. But that is not to say that after the furore has diminished, and insight becomes possible, that ways of coping in an unrestricted environment cannot then be nurtured. If, as I have suggested in this chapter, crisis services are unlikely to thrive as an alternative to hospital in a political climate where risk to the community is uppermost for policy makers, then the scope for their development seems to lie in their managers being involved in the detention issues, as in the case of Liverpool with the Approved Social Workers, in a collaborative way with their hospital counterparts.

It is also necessary to acknowledge some role for hospital psychiatry in the evolution of crisis services, as otherwise one is simply repeating the mistakes of psychiatric hospital closure where the expertise of staff within the institutions was seriously undermined, with implications that are still very much evident in the reprovided services that are evolving. It would thus seem to be essential for those aiming to provide crisis services to try to identify enthusiasts among hospital staff for crisis response ways of working and to set up development processes in which they play a key role in rethinking the nature of DGH responses.

References

Acheson, E.D. (1985), 'That over used word Community!', *Health Trends*, Vol. 17, p. 3.
Baruch, G. (1984), 'Straightening the Bend: Sociological Contributions Towards the Development of Community Mental Health Care', in Reed, J. and Lomas, G. (eds),

Psychiatric Services in the Community: Developments and Innovations, Croom Helm, London.

Bebbington, A.C. and Kelly, A. (1995), 'Expenditure Planning in the Personal Social Services: Unit Cost in the 1980s', *Journal of Social Policy*, Vol. 24, No. 3, pp. 385–411.

Brown, G.W. and Harris, T. (1978), *The Social Origins of Depression: A Study of Psychiatric Disorder in Women*, Tavistock, London.

Brown, P. (1985), *The Transfer of Care*, Routledge and Kegan Paul, London.

DHSS (1975), *Better Services for the Mentally Ill*, HMSO, London.

DHSS (1981), *Care in the Community: A Consultative Document for Moving Resources in England*, DHSS, London.

Forrest, R. and Murie, A. (1991), *Selling the Welfare State: The Privatisation of Public Housing*, Routledge, London.

Garelick, A.I. (1988), 'The Decision to Close an Area Mental Hospital', *Bulletin of the Royal College of Psychiatrists*, Vol. 12, pp. 52–4.

Hunter, D. (1980), *Coping With Uncertainty*, Research Studies Press, Letchworth.

Ingleby, D. (1990), 'Do not adjust your mind ...', *Health Matters*, Issue 3, p. 16.

MIND (1983), *Common Concern: MIND's Manifesto for a New Mental Health Service*, MIND, London.

Ministry of Health (1956), *Report of the Committee of Enquiry into the Cost of the National Health Service* (Guillebaud report), HMSO, London.

Ministry of Health, Labour and Pensions Inter-Departmental Committee (1968), *Report of the Committee on Local Authority and Allied Personal Social Services* (Seebohm Report), HMSO, London.

Oakley, A. (1974), *Housewife*, Harmondsworth, London.

Ramon, S. (ed.) (1992), *Psychiatric Hospital Closure: Myths and Realities*, Chapman and Hall, London.

Ratna, L. (1998), 'Crisis Services: the Barnet Experience', *Alternative Health International*, Vol. 1, No. 1.

Robinson, F. and Abrams, P. (1977), *What We Know About The Neighbours*, Rowntree Trust Research Unit, University of Durham, Durham.

Scull, A. (1996), 'Asylums: Utopias and Realities', in Tomlinson, D.R. and Carrier, J.W. (eds), *Asylum in the Community*, Routledge, London.

Tooth, G.C. and Brooke, E.M. (1961), *Lancet*, Vol. I, Issue 7179, p. 710.

Wallcraft, J. (1996), 'Asylum and help in times of crisis', in Tomlinson, D.R. and Carrier, J.W. (eds), *Asylum in the Community*, Routledge, London.

Index